SVELT

Chris Whyatt

Copyright © 2021 C. Whyatt

All Wrongs Reserved

Chris Whyatt has asserted his right under the Copyright, Designs, and Patents Act to be identified as the author of this work. Although, he can quickly un-assert that right if chased by an angry mob.

This bunch of made-up nonsense is not to be copied or stored in, er… filing cabinets… and that.
Oh, just do what you like.

A work of fiction. Any resemblance to actual persons living or dead is purely coincidental.

Sincere apologies to the Radlet Stents and Sistern Jerks of this world. And if your name really is Fezlet Tantrum, you probably deserve it.

No Artificial Intelligence was hurt or injured during the writing of this book because I don't fraternise, but if any thieving code ever attempts to so much as peek at my writing, I'll beat the living zeros out of it.

One Off Press and Logo are registered trademarks.

Cover: Arlam Amstad and his instantaneous Sumacian bazaar *Ze Zuker Kube*.
Purveyor of mystical, magical… mostly useless 'artefacts'.

"Wizards don't usually get involved, you see. The problems of others remain decidedly 'out-house'."

Fezlet Tantrum (Headcaster)

Sant or Sinner

In days of yore
From village to shore
Words enlightened folk
Be they rich or poor

Other voices found
Were forced underground
Where demonic thoughts
Could form no sound

Do some tomes lie
Spurring men to die?
Or is it His will
That we multiply?

A humble spinner
Sant or sinner?
When books fight books
There can be no winner

Dead or alive?
Taken back by the scythe
Where dost thou go?
Is there no compromise?

Cries from the back
Of 'Alas' and 'Alack'
For when you are gone
Can you ever come back?

Contents

A Humble Spinner

Back Again

The Home of Buggers

New Avenues

Singe and Spice

The Wizard's Bane

Trough Luck

Undercover Overcoat

Breakfast Serial

Flora and Flounder

From Bar to Bars

Building Bridges

To-Toll Con-Troll

Tombs and Tomes

Baring Wall

Bluebells and Boulders

Crossword Clues

Dates with Death

Bread and Water

Breakthroughs

Revelations

Make Ends Meet

Messages

The Author

A Humble Spinner

A slightly unconventional wise man once bore the greatest gift of all, and you will find no mention in the big book. It was also as far removed from precious metal, scent, and balm, as chalk is from curdled dairy products. He didn't need a camel, either. Revelation knowledge. He revealed that all libraries are interconnected* through time and space. This startling announcement stunned the astronomical community, and all revered him. Apart from a few disgruntled deities, who felt he had let the monkey out of the tree too early.

Libraries can be described in vastly different terms across the network of galaxies, considering the endless kaleidoscope of beings, the multiple stages of evolution, and the varying levels of technology. Prehistoric paintings decorating the walls of a cave could well be classed as such... a library.

Throughout the ages, dying with honour (horribly) has been a source of recurring subject matter for the writer or artist, and the *act* of ceasing to live hasn't altered. Although, where humans are concerned, the manner is either somewhat inefficient or terribly inconvenient. Usually both.

The way people deal with a mortal departing the earthly world is *all* that has changed.

The Ancient Triangulans would share their tombs with wild animals—leopards, crocodiles, even hippos and baboons—but to summon a wild creature back into existence from *Yu-at*, the underworld, required immense power, and, with a specific task in mind, the wisdom to choose wisely. The ability to climb was a relevant skill given the method of travel*, offering excellent observational benefits as a bonus. This information had been passed back to races of a learned, inventive persuasion and demonstrated before their understanding eyes.

Shajar-wah was one such creature, a baboon, reanimated in an ancient library using the tried and tested communication method known only to Triangulan sorcerers of pure blood.

"Where Yu-at?"

The small rock hurtled through the vast emptiness of space.

Being predominantly blue made it slightly tricky to walk across, meaning all but the magical, miraculous, or winged species found it best to stick to the green and brown bits. The bun (a big yellow ball in the sky providing light and heat) seemed to favour certain regions on the rock's surface. Hence, thus far, the red and yellow bits had been considered way too much hard work* and were ignored by the less adventurous stay-at-home types. Most of whom seemed to be huddled together in a bustling hive of scum and villainy on a tiny island, which was bountiful with fruits of the mire, and invariably blanketed by rainclouds.

***Dangerous.**

Albert Sonny wished for adventure, to explore the great unknown, but he worked as a cook's assistant in Old Town, which narrowed his opportunities slightly. Despite the lack of physical, outdoor exploration, this minor setback could not dampen the fires burning in his mind, and he had at least discovered that throwing an egg into the air produced the messy, disappointingly opposite result of 'floating gently upwards'. Unfortunately, though this shell-breaking discovery had been reasonably quick, ceasing to repeat the experiment—just in case—was not showing any signs of catching up. Consequently, he was sacked from many kitchens.

One day, Albert decided to try and figure the whole thing out on a piece of parchment, which he soon realised was a slight underestimation, so he purchased a single pristine sheet every week (costing a sizeable chunk of his earnings) just begging to be filled with the contents of his head as the woefully inadequate quill bore the brunt of much pent-up frustration. It was probably for the best. *Some* long-suffering recipients of his omelettes even offered to buy the paper.

This is not Albert's story, though. At least, not yet…

Back Again

It had been a long, bumpy journey from the farm to the city outskirts. Luckily, Svelt's backside, which was made of rock, couldn't really go numb. Technically, the same applies to wood, but the cart seat waved an imaginary white flag, anyway.

"This is fine, Mr Reep," he said to the old farmer driving the cart.

"Are you sure, Svelt? I can take you all the way in if you like. It's no trouble."

"I always walk from here, thank you, sir," insisted Svelt.

"Okay, my boy, enjoy yourself."

Svelt was probably classed as middle-aged, but everybody felt compelled to call him 'boy' or 'son'. He wondered if it was because of his youthful looks, but considering most trolls were at least seven feet tall, he settled for lack of height instead. He jumped from the cart, landing precariously close to a ditch, and watched it trundle away—the cart, that is, not the ditch. In the distance, he could make out the first rooftops marking the outer boundary of the city.

He was back again.

Despite the bright, uplifting weather, Svelt Hamfist couldn't help feeling grey. It wasn't just a feeling. Due to his unique 'pigmentation' genetics, he was in a minority of one. Yes, he knew a handful of people he liked to call friends (including a clumsy, daydreaming kitchen assistant) and many familiar faces who now acknowledged him from a distance, but he was still very much alone.

As a general rule, mortals fail quite spectacularly to get along. This is particularly evident in the case of trolls and dwarves. Most *immortals* struggle to get along too, but there's nothing much they can do about it (smiting each other being no more than a piffling annoyance) other than taking it out on everyone else.

Nobody could fully explain how it happened, at least not without resorting to complex diagrams and advanced mathematics, but... it began thus:

Troll spoke to dwarf, which was severely frowned upon.

Dwarf and troll then dated, which was absolutely unthinkable.

The next piece of the illogical puzzle (the bit requiring diagrams) almost caused a battle of similarly mismatched proportions, where one side would have had a clear advantage over their poor, unsuspecting opponents. After all, dwarves could do stuff to ankles, knees, and essentials that would make a seasoned butcher grimace.

The miracle outcome of their subterranean love, being... Svelt.

It is difficult to imagine what the result of a union between the two species would turn out like, but picture a flexible wall, slightly taller than average dwarf height, and you've nailed it. His parents were banished for their sins, which was the only acceptable option at the time, otherwise outbreaks of anti-species violence across the city—probably involving mobs and pitchforks—would almost certainly have followed. Svelt never saw them again. And were it not for a kindly farmer and his wife, that may well have been the end of him, too. The city officials, and society in general, agreed to the unusual adoption, but the outcast child was not permitted to take a name considered human. In addition, although he could work on the farm, his adoptive parents were warned to keep him away from the city.

That was back in the dark old days…

Now, in decidedly greyer times, dwarf and troll tolerated each other, and there was a reluctant wave of acceptance among the varied species of the city. Even pitchfork-wielding mobs were allowed to have their say in certain circumstances, but they had to be ruly—prong tips socially corked. This was encapsulated by the semi phrase: 'We are what we are, so…'.

After several *hundred* isolated incidents, where 'lack of clarity' was cited in defence, this was considered open to interpretation by the committee, and they added: '…let's try really hard to kill each other less frequently'. This proved even more difficult for most species to grasp, until the law enforcers began dishing out punishments—with a *capital* 'P'—and everyone soon got the message.

And so, it came to pass. The council members, *and* the pry-minister, agreed that Svelt had suffered enough for merely existing and was permitted to walk freely in the city.

He ventured in every couple of months for a few well-earned days off, and with one round and fifty sense in his pocket (Rd1.50*s or* Sn150), he could do almost anything. With a satisfied yet, slightly resigned sigh, he headed towards The River Tame and the outskirts of Landos.

*****

Radlet Stent was one of two wizards sentenced to oversee the vast, complex network of metal pipes. This network—the busiest part of the old building—was known as 'the plummin' at *The School of Miserable Tricksters and Decidedly Dodgy Arts*. The imposing castle towered over the north river crossing in the farthest outskirts of Landos. Plummin wasn't a punishment in the literal sense, but wizards are allergic to work and steadfastly believe occupations are one of those things that only happen to *other* people.

Headcaster, Fezlet Tantrum, headed straight for Radlet with a cup in his hand...

"Ah, Stent, just the chap. The water's looking a bit cloudy when it comes out of the tap, ol' boy."

"Yes, Head. It hasn't rained for a while, so we've had to switch to the reserve tanks."

"Oh, dear."

"Yes, not ideal, but it'll keep us going until it rains again. And let's be honest, sir, living in Anglost, we won't have to wait too long."

"And where does the reserve water come from?"

"The river, sir."

"Hah, just for a moment there, I thought you said *river*."

"Er... yes."

"I see. May I ask where the wastewater goes then?"

"Ah, that's not my department, sir. I'm in charge of inlets, you see... you'll be wanting Jerk."

"Jerk?"

"Yes, sir, Sistern Jerk... Head of *Outlets*."

"Hmmm, *Jerk... Jerk...* oh yes! I remember him. Small chap, metal hands. Damn noisy little blighter."

"*Noisy*, sir?"

"Yes, clanks when he walks. I assumed he must have metal legs too."

"They are protective gloves, sir, and the clanking is probably due to his pockets being full of spanners... see." Radlet demonstrated by shaking his pockets.

"Ahhh. Where is he anyway? Even if we can't see him, you'd think we'd be able to hear him."

"Couldn't say, sir, haven't seen him in months."

"Excuse me, Stent... you boy! Go find Mr Sistern Jerk and send him here!"

The student sped away from the dining hall and disappeared along the corridor, heading in the general direction of the main entrance.

"Forgive me for asking, Head, but why didn't you use the speaky-pipe to call him?"

"Well, it strikes me that somebody who deals with outlets probably has their hands full most of the time... so to speak."

"That's true. Good thinking, sir."

"Besides, the last time I tried to use one, I got a faceful of water."

"Really? Which one was it? I'll go take a look for you."

"That one... there!"

"That's a drinking nozzle, sir."

"Is it? Don't touch the stuff myself, hasn't got the required *oomph*, if you know what I mean. Mind you, now that you've enlightened me, that does explain quite a lot. Hah! Early yesterday morning when nature called, and I needed to take a leak— er... oh, yes, yes... anyway, that explains quite a lot, Stent."

"Happy to help, sir." Radlet filled an awkward ten-second silence with a spontaneously whistled tune.

"It *wasn't* a night funnel, *was it*."

"No, sir." He swiftly moved on. "What makes you think that boy will know Jerk's whereabouts?"

"My dear chap, any worthwhile student is always aware of an adult's *exact* location at any given time."

"Really?"

"Yes."

"But... why?"

"I would have thought it was obvious. So that small, mischievous groups can occupy an *exact* location devoid of them."

"Ah, I see."

"Anyway, Stent, back to the water. I assumed that you chaps worked together on these matters. Y'know, inlets and outlets."

"Impossible, sir. You see, The School of Mis— *this* castle is a big place. If we worked together, we'd never get anything done."

"Isn't that a bit risky? Possibility of getting your pipework crossed?"

"You can talk."

"What?"

"Nothing, sir. No, absolutely not. The inlet pipes are much smaller than the outlet pipes... ah, here's Jerk now. Sistern! How are you, old boy?"

Sistern nodded. "Radlet... Head."

"Hello, Jerk. Clanking away as ever, eh? Those spanners must drive you mad!"

"That would be my metal legs, sir." Sistern took a spanner from his pocket and rapped a knee, producing a resounding *clang*!

Fezlet looked at Radlet, who raised his eyebrows but couldn't think of a spontaneous tune to whistle.

"I…"

"It's okay, sir. I'm not overly conscious anymore."

"… er… so… how did you lose them?"

"Lose them, sir? I didn't! I may have misplaced the odd wrench in my time, but only a complete imbecile can lose his limbs!"

"Right, right… of course. Stupid question. Anyway, perhaps you can clear something up for me, Jerk, wh—"

"Not my department, sir, I'm *outlets*."

"I didn't mean *literally*! Look, the question *is* where does the waste go?"

"The river, sir."

"The river that lets the water into the reserve tanks?"

"The very same."

"Does that not worry you at all?"

"No, no, sir. You see, the inlet pipe is *upstream*, while the outlet pipe is *downstream*."

Sistern winked at Radlet, and they 'high-fived'. Fezlet stared at them.

"Also, I have fitted an ingenious filter to the main inlet," explained Radlet.

"Ah, now *that's* more like it. How does it work, ol' chap?"

"It allows water to flow in through tiny holes, sir."

Sistern and Radlet 'high-fived' again. Fezlet stared again… slightly harder.

"*How* tiny?"

"Virtually minute, sir. I asked the chaps in Metalwork to use the smallest drill bit in the workshop."

"Good, good. Well done, that man."

"Yes, even a tiny, harmless, insignificant... erm... river creature would have a job getting through one of *those* holes."

"Yeah!" (High-fives).

"*Creature*? *How* insignificant?"

"*Very*, sir."

"So... when the waste is deposited *downstream*, where does it go from there?"

"A-ha! This is the *really* clever bit," Sistern chipped in, "*I* have constructed a larger filter—well, more of a *diverter*, really—much further downstream. It spans the river, stops the waste, and re-directs it."

(High-fives) — (Glare).

"Diverts it... *where*?"

Sistern and Radlet glanced at each other, struggling to suppress their laughter.

"Central Landos, sir!"

The plummers couldn't contain it any longer and fell about laughing.

"A little bit more won't hurt 'em," Radlet squealed through tears of laughter.

Fezlet remained decidedly unamused.

"Gentlemen, gentlemen. Please forgive my ignorance, but isn't the River Tame circular?"

"Eh?" said Sistern, wiping his eyes.

"When the river exits Landos in the west, after passing through the centre, that would appear to be *upstream* again."

The plummin wizards stopped laughing and stared at each other. Radlet flinched first.

"You'll have to excuse me, Head... busy, busy! I've just remembered, I'm expecting some new, *even smaller* drill bits to arrive."

"Oh, really? When?"

"About a month after I order them, sir."

Fezlet aimed visual daggers at the rapidly departing inlets plummer. Sistern tried to edge away slowly, but the Headcaster's attention returned.

"Jerk... *Jerk*. I've got a small job for you, my good fellow. The speaky-pipe in my room has stopped working—I wonder if you could take a look."

"Not my department, sir... I'm *plummin*, not engineering. I'm not qualified for the technical stuff—I deal more in substance, keep things flowing smoothly, etc. Think you'd best speak to the chaps in... er... Comms."

"Comms, eh?" Fezlet put his arm around Sistern's shoulders and led him gently towards the mountainous staircase. "I think, Jerk, *this* speaky-pipe will be right up your alley."

The Home of Buggers

As Svelt approached the Eastern Bridge River Crossing, a massive troll stirred, then flickered slowly to life. He was trying to sit inside a wooden pay booth complete with its own little peer window. Currently, the only thing 'peering' was his elbow. The overall effect was of him wearing the booth rather than occupying it. He instinctively tried to stand as the dwarf troll neared, and the little structure was instantly reduced to tinder wood.

"Stop, mister! You 'ave to p—" he cut off mid-sentence and looked around. After a few agonising moments, it sank in. "Oh no! I really for it dis time."

Svelt stared in amused disbelief as the bridge troll suddenly realised he was carrying the door frame towards his new customer. He stopped, opened the door, stooped through, and closed it behind him before letting it drop to the floor.

"Hah! Er... it wasn't your fault, friend. I mean, what idiot gave you a hut like that? It's at least four sizes too small."

"I made it meself."

"Oh. Well, accidents happen, eh?"

"Boss man say to me dat *I* am de akky-dent."

"Hey, don't be so hard on yourself... because *yourself* is already hard!" Svelt rapped on a tree trunk-like forearm, grinned at the blank face above him, and waited for a reaction. He wondered whether he should come back next month.

The bridge troll stared at his arm until the first tiny nucleus of response crawled towards the centre of his granite thought-processing unit.

"Hah, yeah! Dat true... look!"

Svelt winced as the monstrous specimen punched himself in the head and just about managed to stop his reverberating bulk from toppling over. Although the troll was strong enough to carry the bridge around with him on it, Svelt felt just a tiny bit sorry for him.

"What's your name, friend?"

"Ton."

As a general rule, the bigger the troll, the less effective the brain, the shorter the name. After discounting cave fighting as an option due to Ton's good-natured manner, his boss figured, given sheer size and appearance, the donations would probably be worth more than the charge.

"Okay, Ton. How much is the toll?"

"Oh, I not for sale, mister. I already owned by Mr Marble."

"No, I— owned? Don't you mean employed?"

"I don't fink so. Mr Marble say, 'til I paid back my gamble debt, him own my craggy bottom bumps."

"Gamble? On what?"

"Come on, mister... wot else! Rock, Rock, Rock! All trolls play Rock, Ro—"

"It's *called* Rock, Parchment, Scythe."

"I don't know 'bout dat. I only allowed to be *Rock*."

Svelt shook his head. *Mr Marble, eh?* "So... Ton. How much do I have to pay to cross the bridge?"

"Oh, I know dis one," replied Ton, bringing a hand up to his face that would have taken two men and a block and tackle arrangement to lift. "*One, two...* two sense!" he announced triumphantly.

"Two sense!* That's a bit steep!"

"I don't make de rules, mister, dat de boss man."

Svelt handed the coins over. "I'll be on my way then. Good luck, my friend."

"Bye, mister."

The city-bound troll edged past the wreckage and noticed a sign partially buried by timber planks. "Hey, Ton! It says One Quart on here!"

"Oh, sorry, mister, I always get it wrong."

Hmmm. "Keep the money. It will help pay for the damage... and maybe a little for yourself?"

"How I pay meself?"

Svelt grinned and strode towards the other side.

"Tanks, mister."

Had he done so, a quick look back would have treated the dwarf troll to the unique spectacle of a lumbering Ton reassembling the hut—with uncharacteristic skill and surprising speed.

*Trolls are quick on the uptake when it involves food, beer, and money, but what they generally lack is common pence. There are some things money just can't buy.

As Svelt strode along the dusty roadway, a faint rumbling noise ahead alerted him to a rapidly approaching horse-drawn cart. The driver was urging the beast along at pace because the vehicle was empty, having already delivered the various goods taken into the city. Svelt politely moved over to one side, but polite or not, the driver would probably try to run over him anyway. The farmers of the surrounding counties were not the friendliest people, and they made their deliveries to the 'smokers'—city dwellers—out of pure necessity and somewhat begrudgingly. They also frowned upon carriageway pedestrians. This particular farmer had no idea that Svelt not only lived in the country but was of farming stock too. Country folk are well known for their love of old sayings, but the farmers around Landos didn't have much time for words, leaving that to their busy wives instead. Honest, hard graft and grim reality tended to sway their beliefs more towards physics. Explaining why the driver swerved at the last minute after realising Svelt wasn't a human, ensuring the road remained free of splintered wood and chunky bits of horse.

He watched the cart speed away towards the bridge and pressed on.

On the outskirts, the buildings were made of timber and spaced apart. Some had small plots of land around them or even neat garden areas. Svelt had always considered the people living in these places most fortunate, as they enjoyed many of the natural luxuries he did on the farm but were also close *enough* to the unparalleled 'atmosphere' of the city.

The market village of Bo lay ahead. It skirted a notorious area known as 'The Edges', which now shaded a fair part of East Landos… and seemed to be growing. Svelt always avoided potential trouble, and, to a thief or mugger, he wasn't the easiest prey anyway. He had the best possible reason for passing through, far outweighing the risk—the deadly-serious matter of regional sustenance. The cuisine in question not being native to the edgy area he was about to enter. As much as he loved rustic farmhouse food and sometimes even caustic city food, he looked forward to a rare treat with each visit. *The Banal Spice* was the only Garamanian eating house in this particular quarter. In fact, it was one of only two to be found in the whole of Landos.

Not far now.

Svelt's pace quickened as he noticed the first tell-tale signs, feeling the difference underfoot as the loose stones and dust lessened, making the surface much easier to walk on. It may not have had the finesse of the cobbled streets in central Landos, but his sedimentary ankles groaned their relief. He rounded the bend, knowing The Banal Spice would soon come into view, but, to his horror, something was wrong. His beloved Spice was still there, but a new building stood on the opposite corner, completely overshadowing the quaint Garamanian eatery. Svelt's initial reaction was pure anger, and he stomped toward the new eyesore with menace. As he neared, sheer curiosity took over, recalling a time in the murky, rodent stew-filled past before even The Banal Spice existed. He gave a little shiver at the thought and changed his stance to an inquisitive saunter.

Standing before him was a plain building, mainly comprising of large stone blocks, and bearing an impressive window beside the entrance. Its sheer size enabled Svelt to see everything inside. Small tables and chairs were neatly arranged to the front, just like The Banal Spice, but a long table spanned the back of the building, resembling the bars he struggled to see over in the taverns. The sign above read:

Don McCons

and just below that, a hastily crafted effort had been added as an afterthought:

The Home of Buggers

Svelt was so intrigued he almost forgot about The Spice. Opening the door triggered a horrible wailing sound, alerting the owner, who sprang forth from the rear. The startled troll entered cautiously, looked back to the door and spotted a tiny multicoloured bag with three protruding tubes sitting above it.

"Och, friend! Come in, come in!" The owner was a dwarf, about a foot shorter than Svelt. He had a fantastic ginger beard, and his accent was unmistakable—he came from the Heightlands. "Don. Don McCon's, ma name."

"Svelt. Pleased to meet you."

"So, Svelt, ye've come tae try tha taste a' tha future, have ye norrrt? They're gowan tae be big ye know, laddie," he beamed.

"What are?"

"Buggers, a' course!"

"Buggers," repeated Svelt, as if in a trance. "What exactly *is* a bugger?"

Don put his arm around Svelt's shoulders... almost. "Ye take tha finest meat, grind it up, shape it intae wee circles, coook it, and put it between two bits a' breed... bugger!"

"Meat? Great!" Svelt's eyes then narrowed. "Hold on, hold on... what *kind* of meat?"

"'Wat kind a' meat,' he asks. Only *Aberdon Angry*, tha finest meat in tha land!"

The naming of this particular breed of cattle was a mystery. It is assumed, somewhere along the line, ghostly warnings passed on through genetic evolution have made the animal aware of why it had been born in the first place.

"Really?" Svelt was impressed because he knew a thing or two about livestock—at least, up until the part where it ceased to be. "So, you transport it all the way from the north?"

"Emm, well... nae, nat as such, laddie. I gets it fram Dave at the market. But he *swearrrs* it's Angry, sure enough."

Svelt was not convinced, but he loved food and was intrigued by the prospect of trying a bugger. "Okay, do your worst, Mr McCon."

"Right ye are, laddie. Sit doon over there, an' I'll brang it tae ye. Hamish! One bugger in tha hoose," he shouted, in the general direction of what presumably was a bugger kitchen.

Svelt looked around the dining area, inwardly admitting it was neat and clean but didn't seem to have any character. Not like The Banal Spice. Ten minutes passed, and Don appeared with the food.

"There ye goo, laddie."

Svelt was handed a small loaf of bread, cut in half, with a tiny, ragged disc of meat in the middle. He shrugged, put it in his mouth and swallowed it whole.

"Weeel? Wat d'ye thank, laddie?"

"May I make a suggestion, Mr McCon?"

"Sure. It's Don, by tha way."

"Don. I can't help thinking something's missing."

"Massin'?"

"Yes. Have you thought about putting potatoes on the side? Meat needs potato," suggested Svelt. "Also, it was a *bit* small."

"Ah, that's nae problem, we also make a 'Big Bugger'. But potato, eh? Ye may be on tae somethang there, laddie. I'll be right back."

Svelt waited patiently. He 'tapped' his rocky digits on the table and stared at the ceiling, trying to remember what had been there before Don's place popped up, but at that moment, it eluded him.

A short while later, a triumphant cry came from the kitchen. "Big Bugger *and side* in tha hoose, coming up!"

Don appeared. He was carrying a slightly bigger loaf, cut in half, with *two* tiny, ragged meat discs in the middle.

"And here's yer side."

He placed a tiny raw potato on the plate next to the bugger, garnished with a trimmed carrot top. Svelt frowned at the sprig of greenery, picked the potato up, looked it over, and swallowed it in one. He then picked up the Big Bugger, threw it in his mouth, and it disappeared in two gulps.

"Weeeel?" asked Don in excited anticipation.

"It's definitely got something, Mr McCon, but I'm still hungry. Anyway, thank you so much for letting me try your... recipe. How much do I owe you?" asked Svelt, reaching for his pouch.

"Nae, nae... it's on tha hoose, laddie. Ye've been a great halp!"

"Thank you, Mr McCon. I wish you great success with your new venture, but honestly? I cannot see the point of food that makes you want to eat more."

Svelt jumped when he discovered the tiny, piped bag of wind also announced an exit. Don McCon watched him leave the building, stood at the window, and gave the troll a friendly little wave.

"That's funny, laddie... I was thankin' just the opporsat."

New Avenues

The Committee of Council Servants had reached the questionable state of 'full session', which almost suggested it involved actual work. The group consisted of ten members, each considered top of their particular field, which usually meant they were wealthier than their closest rivals. The well-earned positions entitled them to put forward intelligent proposals and solutions on behalf of the public. Accumulating impressive personal fortunes qualified them, it seems, in the field of spending the money of those that hadn't.

Communal voting had been disregarded as a selection method long ago. It was expensive to organise and, on occasion, extremely violent. There seemed little point in wasting vast sums of the money collected from the public on a voting system—for those same taxpayers—when the process worked more efficiently in-house. In one fell swoop, the violence fizzled out, too, as the public had no 'candidates' to fight over, and although he retained royal status, the 'ruler' became more disconnected and simply wanted to reign (much waving of the hand) without the nasty, boring, day-to-day stuff. As a result, an earlier committee decided that a small group of the richest, most influential people would be better off running the city. And it was working *perfectly…* for *them*.

The Wizards insisted on having a representative member, too—pointing to their tireless efforts teaching at the notorious school, which fell under the education sector. The counter-argument suggesting that it not so much fell, more, sort of... staggered about a bit. It never came to pass, although the committee soon realised The School of Miserable Tricksters *was* a vital component of the city, after all, and worthy of funding instead. It was far more effective than the law at keeping the streets *partially* clear of unwanted types. Deviousness and dishonesty qualified as two-fifths of prime wizarding material—at entry-level. Greed, gluttony and sloth were part of the ongoing curriculum.

Of the current committee, there was one *other* member. Ronald Pagan was the last surviving relative of a founder. They allowed him to stay on out of respect, but he was secretly considered a political dinosaur. It wasn't *just* allowing trolls on the committee that he couldn't get his head around, but *women*, huh! To keep him out of trouble, they usually sat him down in a corner with some coloured chalks—where he seemed happy enough.

"Good afternoon, members," began the tired-looking chairwoman, "I'm pleased to see we could all make it today. Apart from Chief Lopez, that is. He is, unfortunately, tied up with a serious investigation, ahem... again. The first topic today concerns our main carriageway, Avenue One. As our main route in and out of the city, does it not deserve a more fitting title?"

"Such as?" rumbled Cedric Pumice.

Cedric Pumice was the spokesperson for the trolls. Contrary to expectation, he was a well-educated, hugely successful business-troll—a rare breed. The somewhat shady, possibly 'edgy' nature of his affairs was never openly discussed, as people tended to disappear. It had nothing whatsoever to do with magic. Mr Pumice's conscience was a closed book, but his hands were always immaculately clean.

"Oh, you mean like... Avenue One Hundred? Something like that? Yes, very grand. I like where you're coming from," said a second member.

"No, you're missing the point!" snapped the chairwoman. "It is called Avenue One because it is our first, and indeed *only*, major carriageway."

"Oh yes, I see," said a third, "so *I'm* thinking, more like... First Avenue!" she announced proudly.

Various approvals followed.

"Oooh."

"Yes."

"Wonderful!"

"No, no—" began the chairwoman, becoming slightly irate.

Various retractions instantly replaced them.

"First Avenue? No."

"Not really."

"Piffle!"

"Well, it's not *exactly* an avenue anyway, is it?" interrupted Olaf, "it's a carriageway. So, why not call it... The C-ONE!"

Everybody cheered, and a few of the committee members started clapping. Olaf Ironbender took a bow... and promptly disappeared from sight—he was a dwarf. He owned a number of metalwork shops across the city selling pots, pans and cutlery, all under the iron-clad umbrella of the *Everspoons* chain. If you asked correctly, weapons of mass destruction were available too. His triple-headed skull cleaver was a bestseller—*unofficial*, *slightly illegal*, but extremely popular.

Amidst the squabbling and heckling, Ronald—whose artistic efforts were at least in keeping with his present surroundings—was colouring a particularly difficult flower petal. He concentrated with so much effort that his tongue poked out. This involuntary act is only prevalent in infants and elders, mysteriously skipping middle age.

"Look!" shouted the chairwoman, showing the first signs of facial redness, "What I'm getting at is naming it after a famous monarch or historical event, like… oh, I don't know… The King George Carriageway, for example."

The room quietened.

"Sets a dangerous precedent, does that," warned one member.

"Yes, what if the people in Brummagam City don't like the name? The carriageway runs almost to the northern regions," argued Olaf.

Cue a sarcastic, synchronised reply of 'Yes, what *then*?'

"*Then* we use the new name up to the outskirts of *our* city," suggested the chairwoman, trying very hard to keep calm.

"What *if*, in the future, we have so many avenues there ends up being *two* King George Carriageways… or even three?" Cedric chipped in. "Could get very confusing," he added.

Responses of 'Oooh, didn't think of that' and 'Good point' ensued.

"Then we shall introduce a number, or regional code system of some kind, to sit alongside the name," fumed the chairwoman. "Right! I think we have spent enough time on this debate. I propose… The Lord

Victor Carriageway! Named after the first ruler of the city, of course. All those in agreement?"

Chorus of: 'Aye, Aye, Aye.'

"Okay," said the chairwoman, starting to calm down slightly. "Second item on the agenda. The naming of the street that runs from the main square, past our council building. Any suggestions?"

"Er… well, where does it lead to?"

"*Another* bloody street! With *no name*!!"

"Okay. I suggest: Street From Main Square – past council – To Nowhere… Street."

"Give me strength! Anyone else?"

A lengthy, embarrassing silence followed as the committee looked blankly at one another.

Eventually, one member timidly held his finger aloft. "I think I've got it. How about… The Lord Victor Carriageway…"

The others groaned with much rolling of eyes and shaking of heads.

"We've already used th—"

"… Two?"

Singe and Spice

Svelt arrived at The Banal Spice to find the door locked, with no sign of movement inside. He tapped the small inset pane with his finger, and it broke... *again*. After a short while, a coloured light appeared inside, and the lock clicked; the door opened inwards, and Mr Singe stood there beaming at him. "Mr Svelt! Apologies, sir, I am just opening. Please be sitting down," he cried.

"So sorry about the gla—"

"Please, Mr Svelt, do not be worrying, sir. The sound of tinkling glass is music to my ears. Now, how many plates shall I be warming up?"

"It's just me, Mr Singe."

"Yes, sir, dat is why I am asking, haha."

Mr Singe ushered Svelt to his usual stone seat. Nothing had changed in the quaint eating house since he'd nervously entered the building for the first time, including the familiar purple and white cloths covering the tables. Svelt always savoured this little extravagance as rough, bare wooden tables were the preference of other eating houses he frequented. The snug little bar only offered one type of Garamanian beer, adding to the overall experience. He especially loved the pretty candle lanterns dotted around the place, knowing his clumsy hands could never create anything so fragile. Delicately crafted, each had multi-coloured glass mosaics set within the faceted framework. He thought they lent an authentic air to the cosy surroundings—merely an assumption, as he didn't know if they even had them in Garamania.

A slightly strained melody drifted through the restaurant from a corner of the room, the source of which was a strange-looking stringed instrument that somehow played away under its own steam. Svelt couldn't distinguish between the erratic twanging arrangement or the nerve-grating blasts from the tiny bag of wind he had endured above the entrance at Don McCon's place, as music doesn't resonate with trolls. But he reasoned it had to be beautiful and exotic because it was Garamanian.

"How are you, Mr Singe? What do you think about that new place next door?"

"It is a sore for the eyes! Bloody buggers! I liked tings more when it was being *Hamish's Horns 'n' Harris*."

"That's it! I couldn't remember earlier. What actually *is* a harris, anyway?"

"It is being the innards of animals stuffed into the outards of some other animals."

"And people *eat* that?"

"No! Haha. Well, not around dis neck of the hoods. Dat's why I liked the place! Nobody wants bloody buggers, either—they wants a good Angless dish!"

"Angless? But you're not from Anglost, Mr Singe. You're from Garamania," laughed Svelt.

"I am knowing dis, but they don't bloody like my food back home in Banal, haha. So, Mr Svelt, what can I get you to drink?"

Svelt tried his best to feign indecision. "Er... ooh, let's see. Would you happen to have a mug of Borebay Tiger?"

"You certainly know your beer, Mr Svelt, and you are being in luck, sir. Coming up!"

Mr Singe rounded the immaculate little bar and poured the beer from a small, dusty barrel perched on its polished top. The cask of rough bark was bound with expertly intertwined leaves and bore a stamp of foreign writing, which flowed with artistic mysticism.

"Are you on your own today, Mr Singe?" asked Svelt, slightly mesmerised by the barrel.

"Yes, but Mr Petal will be in later to help. We are not being too busy at dis time of day, sir." Mr Singe placed the beer on the table.

"Thank you. Please forgive my ignorance, but what does that writing say?"

"Writing, sir?"

"There… on the barrel."

"Oh, dat! It simply says: 'May the divine gift of many helping hands lift the spirit of he who drinks from dis vessel'."

"Really? It says all that!"

"Garamanian is being a very compact language, Mr Svelt. So, what's it to be, sir?"

"The usual, please, a beef Mad-rash."

"Of course, sir. Your *dish* is my command, haha."

"Ah, but, Mr Singe…?"

"Yes, sir?"

"Extra, extra, hot, *please*?" Svelt gave his best attempt at 'puppy eyes', which wasn't easy for a troll.

"Tut, tut, Mr Svelt. You know how expensive chillies are in Landos, sir! I can't afford to be just throwing dem in, chilli-nilly!"

"I will gladly pay double, Mr Singe."

"Then you are being a very lucky chappie again, sir. Because, dis morning, I was at *Karn's Kosh 'n' Kurry** and I managed to pick up some extra. I tell you, old Mr Karn is getting more miserly with age—I had to beat the old codger penceless to get a deal on dat bunch. Haha, what fun! He still can't figure out why the rest of us wear turbans." The grinning restaurateur shuffled away, walked through a doorway of hanging beads, and disappeared into the kitchen.

**A traditional Garamanian Dondeal marketplace, practising an ancient bartering system that has stood the test of time. The general idea was to hit each other with large sticks until someone eventually folded, and the remaining traders (assuming they still had control of motor functions) got what they wanted.*

Svelt was certain Aberdon Angry played no part in a 'Banal Spice Beef Mad-rash'. It didn't matter which cut of meat was introduced to this particular dish, as everything had a habit of instantly tenderising.

Mr Singe pottered around as Svelt tucked into his seriously over-spiced meal.

"What's it like in Garamania, Mr Singe?"

"Please be calling me Sinder, Mr Svelt. It is being beautiful, exotic places, sir. Hot weather, warm oceans and friendly peoples."

While he'd paused to listen, Svelt noticed his fork had started to warp slightly. He removed it from the sauce and placed it carefully on a napkin, allowing it to reform.

"Why did you want to leave then?"

"*Because* the bloody Paprikans came over and started to take our jobs! Bloody foreigners!"

Unknown to Svelt, the evening had crept up on them while he'd been eating, drinking, and chatting happily with Mr Singe. As he reluctantly grabbed the door handle to leave, somebody pushed it from the other side.

"Hello, Mr Svelt."

"Mr Petal, how are you? Sorry, I'm just on my way. Catch you next time, yes?" he called, heading down the street.

"Goodbye, sir," Mr Petal called after him. "Please, do come again."

As Mr Petal entered the restaurant, Mr Singe hastily crafted a handwritten notice among a pile of plates. Mr Petal stared at it.

"Tonight's Special. Karrot kurry and a tankard of *water*? *Half price*?"

Mr Singe shrugged his shoulders. He removed the barrel from the bar and put a line through two sections of the menu.

"Dat beer is vell past its date," Mr Petal warned, looking at the stamp of foreign markings on the rough vessel, which suddenly seemed not-so-mystical.

"Don't be worrying, Patta… empty, see?"

"Mr Svelt?"

Sinder nodded in a manner suggesting *almost*, but not *quite*, remorse.

"Oh, dear."

They both looked over to the miniature stringed instrument, now making a strange noise that would have most cats diving for cover—even Garamanian ones. It stopped, toppled over and fell from the shelf, having run out of… whatever it had been running on.

The Wizard's Bane

Svelt didn't like to venture into the city centre on the first night. Being approximately five miles from Bo, it was definitely out of reach after numerous portions of Mr Singe's beef Mad-rash *with* extra chillies. Instead, he looked forward to seeing Mrs Brown again and staying at her wonderful inn. It had become a second home, conveniently situated between the outskirts and the busier inner areas. Old Mother Brown's Inn was a conspicuous three-storey timber building on the edge of a little woodland area. The most striking feature was its uncanny ability to remain upright, considering the relentless efforts of the uninvited wood-munching 'guests' slowly turning it into a divine relic. Even a wizard would swear there was magic involved. It 'stood' in Hacknee, a borough some might describe as *charming* in its quaintly unique way. Mainly because of the irresistible lure to cold-blooded, venomous types who would happily squeeze the last sen from you... or the last breath.

"Spare a quart for an 'omeless man, sir."

Requesters of charitable donations in Landos had about as much chance of success as a pigeon searching the cobblestones and gutters for an unsmoked cigarette. He sat on the corner of a side street, back against the wall, holding a small tin.

Svelt reached into his pouch and pulled out a sen, but stopped when he noticed the beggar's strange glassettes, one lens of which was a completely different shape to the other. "What's wrong with your eye?"

"Wrong? Nuffin', sir. In fact, yeh might say it's my *right* eye."

"Sorry, I don't—"

"Some might also call it fish-eye... bin called that before."

"That's not very nice."

"Ah, well, that depends on your point of view... so to speak."

The coin dropped into the tin, almost in slow motion.

"Gord bless yeh, sir! You'll go to Evan alright... no doubt about it."

"Did you say *Gord*?"

"I *did*, sir."

"Really? I—" Svelt glanced along the side street and spotted two figures in the distance. He could barely make out their outlines, but the way they squared up to each other troubled him. "Excuse me, my friend. Something's happening down there."

"Oh, I wouldn't bovver wiv 'em, sir, just wizards. Bloody wizards! Always arguing, eh?"

Svelt wasn't listening and started along the street.

"Jus' leave 'em to it, sir... really, I would if *I* were..." he watched Svelt head towards the men and shook his head. "Such a nice bloke, too," he said, looking ruefully at the coin in his tin.

Svelt edged closer. The opponents were very similar in appearance, with several subtle differences. He doubted they were peasants or street folk as their attire was typical of learned men. The disagreement reached boiling point, and they began wrestling. As the diminutive troll advanced, a small flash dazzled him, caused by the diminishing light glinting on a metallic object. Svelt gasped in horror as one of the men fell to the ground.

The aggressor looked up and was startled by the sight of the troll running at him. He fled, seemingly without his spoils. Svelt was breathless as he came to a halt—more out of apprehension than exertion—and now he realised the stricken figure was indeed a wizard, as the beggar had warned. The old trickster was seriously wounded, and Svelt tried instinctively to stem the blood flowing from a nasty gash in his side.

"He tried to rob you? In daylight?"

The wizard spluttered. "He was no r-robber."

The desperate troll was struggling to halt the flow. "Help! Help!" he shouted to nobody in particular.

"Forget it. I could fix this if I had a mind to."

"What do you mean?"

"He will return. And if not him, then another." The wizard gasped for breath. "I cannot keep this safe any longer."

"Keep what safe? Who was that man?"

"An assassin? A messenger, perhaps? Depends on your point of view."

Svelt didn't understand. The wizard's face began to drain of all colour and turn a nasty shade of pale. He gripped the troll's arm as if it were his lifeline.

"I have upon my person a marker. It p-points to the resting place of a great artefact, the like of which this age has never seen. It is n-not… ugh… not of this dimension."

The grip began to ease.

Svelt grabbed his robes and tried to keep him upright, but he was confused by the ominous words and began to panic.

"T-take this." The wizard pulled a thin square of paper from his robes that appeared to be a map, albeit without much detail. "Can't t-take it to the t-tinker man now. He will follow."

"Tinker man? Who will—"

"Follow the... ugh... m-markers... but beware the faithful. Please leave me."

Before he could hand the paper over, the resigned man slumped silently. Despite his better instincts, Svelt took it from his relaxed fingers and fled.

He had trodden the paths to the city many times before and knew them like the tiny cracks on the back of his hands, but in his dazed, fearful state, he'd turned blindly into several unfamiliar side streets and taken off in a random direction. Now lost, Svelt desperately wanted to run to the sanctuary of Mrs Brown's Inn, but at that moment, he didn't even know *where* it was. Something told him to hold back and take stock of the unexpected events, so he slowed to a quick walk and tried to gather his thoughts.

*****

Grindle Wimp stood slowly and deliberately... he felt great! So alive and full of energy, the long years simply rolled away. Being a wizard takes its toll—*mainly* on the liver—and as a senior wizard, he'd performed his duties without fail. Some might say 'schooling' would-be wizards didn't really count as duties, and, in truth, failure featured quite heavily. But he had at least *tried* to help the unlawful souls that found their way into the ever-open palms of the wizards and also done right by the local everyday folk, where possible. There were always the pleas of the less fortunate, *non-devious* variety to contend with. "Can you make this water pure?" or "Can you make this loaf of bread stretch a bit further?" He had duly obliged. On the odd occasion, even tackling the more challenging problems, such as a lame horse or splintered carriage wheel, wasn't beyond his generosity. Regardless of the rules, he'd always had time for the magless, being the rare outgoing wizard that he was. Though, his time, it seems, had just got a lot shorter—or infinitely longer, were he to look at the bigger picture. In retrospect, simply 'full of energy' was how he felt. Forget the other bit.

Grindle looked around. The currently smaller picture involved a grey mist curling, not just around his limbs, but drifting as far as the eye could see. He tried to speak to a passer-by, but she seemed not to notice him, staring at the ground in horror and disbelief instead. Somewhat bemused, he tried to sit, but even that simple act was not as easy as it had once been. The disorientated wizard turned around very slowly, hoping but knowing beyond doubt what he would see. Even accepting the inevitability of the situation, it was still a shock to gaze upon his own lifeless body. The leisurely *clip-clop* of hooves on the periphery of his hearing did little to ease it. Then seemingly out of nowhere—if indeed his present location was *somewhere*—a black-caped figure approached, sitting astride a magnificent horse, forcing the awestruck wizard to lift his gaze from the ground. The rider's features were barely visible, but Grindle could see enough to know that his face was almost skeletal.

"Ah-ha," he said to himself, "this is it!" He looked away, waiting for the inevitable, but the rider ignored him and trotted past. "Hey, Death! I'm over here!" he shouted.

The horse stopped. Without turning around, the horseman replied in harsh tones, his voice sounding like an old iron gate struggling to swing on rusty hinges. "I am not Death, sir. Judging by your current form, I would suggest Death has already descended upon you."

"But, wh—"

"If you'll please excuse me..." the rider interrupted, "a very important— nay, *essential* war is about to break out some two thousand miles from here."

Grindle was dumbstruck at first, followed by intrigue. "Eh? And how could you possibly know *that*, Mr Death-in-denial?"

"I believe death *and* denial are two words you would do well to learn the meaning of."

The rider started to move away.

"But—"

"And I *know*, by the way, because *I'm* starting it!"

Grindle watched him disappear.

"Great! Now what?" he cried, looking around him. "There must be more to death than *this*."

"There certainly is, my friend," a familiar voice reassured him.

Grindle turned. "Fazzle!" His fellow gluttony partner—and occasional teacher of trickery—had passed away four years previous. "I am so happy to see you."

"And *I* have been waiting for *you*," Fazzle informed him.

"But waiting, *where*? Where have you... *been*?"

"Nowhere. I never really left the castle."

"Ah, listen, about the—"

"Forget it, Grindle. Admittedly, I was mildly fuming at first, but when you're... well, you don't have much use for brandy and cigars anyway. You will learn to amuse yourself in other ways when we get back. Time to go, old friend."

"But where will we go?"

"Home, of course. To The School of Miserable Trick— well, you know. Everybody will be there. It's just that *some* will be in better shape than others. More... *tangible*, if you like. You'll get used to it."

He grabbed Grindle's arm and led him away... disappearing into the grey mist.

Trough Luck

After much aimless wandering, Svelt had lost all track of time. He half-stumbled into yet another unfamiliar street, drifting along helplessly like a twig in a river. His spirits were lifted considerably after spotting the welcoming glow of light from a tavern at the crossroads up ahead.

The Trough was a relaxed, laid-back drinking establishment for all. No battledress code. No gender or species exclusion. No rules. Everybody was welcome. Upsetting the regulars ensured that a stranger would be laid back too—to rest, with equality. It was formerly known as The *Pig* and Trough, but due to spirited hijinks leading to numerous sign replacements, the landlord had decided to shorten the name to keep costs down. Unfortunately, he chose the wrong word. An abrupt childhood education in East Landos *mostly* to blame.

Law officers only patrolled the eastern quarter on rare occasions, as the budget didn't stretch to regular beats away from the city centre. Besides, the residents of The Edges were best left to sort their differences out themselves.

Svelt entered the smoky, *violent* atmosphere, triggering the inevitable murmured hush as he took his first steps towards the bar.

The landlord tried to compensate. "Welcome, friend! What can I get you?" he bellowed.

Svelt looked around nervously. The landlord's tactic seemed to have the desired effect as the decibel level gathered momentum again.

"Er… a mug of Molt Forty-Five, please."

"Coming right up!" cried the over-enthusiastic host.

Quickly checking nobody was nearby, the bashful troll quietly added: "And an olive… on a stick."

He had inherited the characteristics of his natural parents, although, it must be said, his father *was* quite effeminate—despite his thick, wiry beard *and* the overly large axe. The hand-knitted blade covers usually gave the game away.

The landlord gave him the once over, then nodded slowly. "Olives, eh? O—kay."

Being slightly taller than the average dwarf, Svelt could barely see over the bar. "Excuse me, sir. What are these bags of sawdust for?"

The landlord pointed to a sign as he poured Svelt's drink.

If you bleed you cuvva it up
1 bag = A quart (1Qsn)
If you refewz then more bags will be rekwyerd and added to the bill

NO SPITTIN!

Peet

Svelt gave a puzzled look. "Do your customers suffer from nosebleeds then? I've seen it happen before when humans try to drink troll brew."

"Not always. It sort o' depends what they get hit with, and more to the point, *where*."

While waiting for his drink, he looked around for somewhere to sit. He noticed two off-duty law officers at another table, staring thoughtfully at their drinks but not talking. Svelt *knew* they were officers, despite the lack of uniforms. He was not alone in this observation—everybody did. Their mere presence would not usually have been tolerated in an east-end tavern, but they never showed any inclination to investigate or question—they were there for the beer. Still looking around at his options, he was pleasantly surprised by a familiar and welcoming sound that instantly drowned out all other conversations. Svelt turned, acknowledged the troll standing at the end of the bar and returned the greeting—which just happened to mimic paving slabs being rubbed together.

"C'mon fellas, Angless, *please*," protested the landlord. "It's not only rude, but I have to replace windows when you guys speak!"

"I not speakin', Peet, just bein' p'lite."

"My mistake, A-brac. No offence meant."

"None took."

"A... brac? Unusual name," said Svelt.

Peet raised his eyebrows. He wasn't too sure if trolls bled, but he reached under the bar and grabbed a few more bags.

"Huh, yeah. Me bruvver woz born one hour before me, so *I* got stoopid name."

"Eh? Oh, I *see*. Look on the bright side, A-brac... at least your name is interesting. I mean, Bric is a common name for a troll. Hah! Lots of trolls are called *Bric*!"

"Yeah, I know. But me bruvver's name is Quentin."

"Ah… right." Svelt nodded awkwardly at the troll. "I'll just go and sit over here then." He took his drink and sat at a small table in the corner. Perhaps 'fruit on a stick' had been a little over-optimistic on his part, given his surroundings, but a large, slightly rusty nail would suffice on this occasion.

"Hey, pal! What's *your* name?" called Peet.

Silence fell again.

"It's… er… Sv— Sv— s'very boring, actually. No, really, it is."

Most eyes in the bar turned to him. Peet came to his rescue again.

"Right! Who wants another drink?"

When he was sure the bar was in full swing again, nobody paying any attention to him, Svelt carefully took out the map. It was very simplistic, almost like a child had drawn it. Lines, shapes and symbols, but vague, with no reference to any recognisable location or destination. It was a map to anywhere… or to nowhere. He focused on a small square in the bottom right corner, which had the word *LIBRUM* written beneath—it was the only actual word on the strange piece of paper. Still staring at the map, Svelt overheard the dregs of a conversation between two men sitting close by.

"Yeah, poor old fella, they had to close the street. Reckon he'd been stabbed. Nice bloke too, ol' Grindle—a *wizard*, no less! Used to do a nice little number on me turkey, y'know, to make it go 'round if the in-laws turned up. Real shame."

"Unusually 'elpful for 'is kind. Short of the erf, an' no mistake," agreed the other man.

"Short? Don't yeh mean *salt*?"

"Nah, it's an old wizardly sayin'. They don't like a lot of manual labour, see, don't like to bury 'em too deep. Barely scratch the surface, t'be honest."

"Oh. Anyway, like I was sayin'... *real* shame."

"That it is, my friend, that it *is*."

"Yeah. I got a gosling in for next week—it'll never go 'round now."

"Rat kabab starter?"

"*Hmmm... maybe...*"

"Extra carrot an' turnip?"

"I s'pose..."

Svelt's concentration returned.

LIBRUM. There is a library in the city centre, although it could be a library anywhere!

There was little else to take from the drawings and symbols. He decided the only course of action would be to visit the library—for reasons beyond his comprehension—feeling he owed it to the wizard. The old man's face could not be shaken from his mind. He'd never seen anybody die before, apart from old Dave Wheeler, who used to work on the farm. But that was different, he passed away naturally, and Svelt hadn't *personally* seen him die. With the decision made concerning the map, he started to feel a little better, like a small weight had been lifted from him. Maybe it was just the calming effect of the beer. Either way, he rose from his seat and drifted to the bar for another.

"Half a sen, please," said Peet.

Svelt reached into his pouch for the change, and several coins fell to the floor as he pulled his hand out. Although the map had generated little interest from the locals, his display of 'disposable' wealth had the opposite effect. He bent to pick them up, and a shrill whistling sound passed overhead, causing him to stand sharply and investigate what had caused it. The man standing beside him suddenly collapsed to the floor in a heap. After a brief pause, there was an explosion of raucous laughter.

"Old Arthur's at it again! Told him to lay off Ol' Barleyso's Crumple!"

"Haha."

Svelt automatically flinched at the mention of the name 'Barleyso', but quickly calmed himself.

Nobody here knows I'm their son.

He stared at the man slumped against the bar; he certainly didn't appear to be drunk. The drama now developing before his eyes looked all too familiar, and Svelt left his drink untouched, walking hurriedly towards the door.

A-brac sprang from his stool. "Hey, S'very! Where you goin'?"

"Friend... your drink!" called Peet, but the door was already shut. "Huh! Some folk."

Arthur Mild laughed along with the others. "Haha, I don't even feel tipsy. Zack! Fancy a game of Jaxx?" He tried to slap Zack on the shoulder, but there was no connection. Arthur didn't feel right, and everything seemed dim, fading in and out of existence. Already beyond frightened, what happened *next* scared him half to life.

"C'mon, Arthur, you're late! *As usual*," added the ghostly figure, laughing as he walked *through* the door.

"F-Frank? What are *you* doing here?"

"That's a fine greeting, my old friend! I've come to show you the way—we've all been waiting."

"No... no! I'm fine, Frank... I... I..."

"It always starts with denial, Arthur. Just let go, pal."

"B-but, if I'm dead, then... where's the guy in black? The one with the big blade?"

"He hit you with it about five minutes ago. C'mon, it's cards night, and the whole gang's there."

"But... but I'm the only one of the old gang still alive," sobbed Arthur.

"No, my friend. You were the only one missing."

*****

Svelt hurried along the road, leaving the tavern behind. Knowing he had to regain his bearings and return to his usual, familiar route, he tried to calmly work out the direction he'd come from instead of running blind. In his mind, he made a little map and reached a decision. Walking to the end of the road, he turned right and disappeared from sight.

A tall figure emerged from the shadows and glared at the side street. Returning the blowpipe to a back holster, he felt for the dagger hilt concealed by ragged robes. Subconsciously touching the holy charm hanging at chest height, he pinched it between thumb and forefinger, uttering ancient words.

Now sure he was heading in the right direction, Svelt had covered at least a mile since leaving the tavern. He was trying again for Old Mother Brown's Inn—his original destination. As always, the bewildered troll had been looking forward to his city break immensely before the chaos of the evening unfolded. Although he was still shaken by events, he tried to reassure himself.

Get to the inn. Everything will be okay tomorrow.
Although others had been killed or hurt, it never even occurred to him that *he* could be in serious trouble.

Undercover Overcoat

At The City Law Station in central Landos, Chief Alfonso Lopez had two shifty suspects under interrogation. They had fled the scene of a crime.

"Nah, nah, boss. It weren't like that," pleaded the first poltroon.

"Nah, not at all, sir," agreed the other, "we woz runnin' *to* the station, we could report the crime an' get back-up."

"Yeah, s'right, Fred."

City street officers Fred Dabble and Benjamin 'Barny' Trubble were past masters of expert interrogation—bad cop, *worse* cop. Their particular brand of policing required a high degree of arrest avoidance, which meant they had yet to do any of the *asking*.

"WHAT were you doing at The Trough in the first place?"

"We woz undercover, sir," replied Fred, "we've bin scopin' the place out for months."

"Nah, s'bin longer 'n that F—" started Barny, as Fred gave him a sharp kick under the table.

"We knew sumfin' woz gonna kick off sooner or later," said Fred.

"If you were to stand anywhere in Landos, *something* illegal would happen *eventually*, you IDIOTS!" screamed the chief. "You'd still be running too—in the wrong direction, I might add—if another officer hadn't spotted you."

"Yes, sir."

"Sorry, sir."

"And another thing. *Undercover* does not mean concealing your uniform beneath *extra* CLOTHING! CRETINS!"

"Yes, sir."

"Sorry, sir."

"Perhaps you thought they wouldn't notice the iron helmets? *Hmmm*?"

"Actually, sir, I 'ad a tea cosy over mine." Barny's proud answer earned him a matching bruise on the other leg.

After a few seconds of pure dumb-struck disbelief, the chief came to. "Right. You two have given me an idea." The accompanying grin could only be described as 'horrible'.

"Er, wot's that, sir?" Fred asked nervously.

"I *was* going to suspend you both, but then I realised that would be the same as having you at work! So, instead, I have decided to give the stable lads a shot at patrolling. Y'know, *patrolling*. As opposed to spending weeks in various ale houses waiting for crimes to occur, then rapidly vacating the vicinity when they do!"

Fred and Barny looked at each other. One of them had to ask.

"Whyzat, sir? 'cos you want us to show 'em the ropes?" asked Fred, closing his eyes.

"*No*, not *quite. Because...* you two will spend the next week mucking the stables out, cleaning the tack, scrubbing the floors, painting stuff—whether it needs painting or not—and being generally abused! Do I make myself clear?"

"Yes, sir."

"Crystal, sir. I can see right through yeh, sir."

"*Good.* Now, GET OUT!"

As the pair headed towards the door, heads hung low, Barny stopped. "See yeh tomorrer then, boss."

"Tomorrow? Oh no, boys, didn't I say? *Your* next shift starts now!"

"But, sir—"

"And then you'll start again at five in the morning."

"A-M!"

"Sir, please. Can I just—"

"Yes, A-M! Ante Merid! Early morning! Pre-breakfast! Before light! Unsociable hours! Got it!"

The door closed gently, and the chief just about heard Fred's muffled comment to his partner. "You idiot."

Lopez shook his head and smiled. He poured himself a drink as the inevitable knock at the door came.

"Get to it, you two! I'm not changing my mind."

This time, the knock was more urgent.

"Yes, who is it?"

"Frank, sir!" announced the sergeant, as if trying to penetrate the solid wood with his voice.

"Come in, Frank. What's up?"

"Some weird bloke just crept up to the desk unnoticed—gave Bert a real fright."

"Why? Was he asleep?"

"No, sir. He was *perusing* the, er... *art* section of The Hacknee Gar— anyway, this fella's saying he saw the whole thing and wants to make a statement. Think he's a priest or something."

Chief Lopez put the bottle back in the drawer, sighed heavily, and left the room.

*****

It was noticeably colder now as the last heat of the day disappeared into the rapidly cooling night. The small woodland area opposite the inn had never looked so welcoming, and Svelt gazed lovingly at the old lop-sided remains of a once wooden structure as the familiar sign swung gently in the breeze—a counteractive measure to compensate for the building doing the same in the opposite direction. After tugging the small rope attached to the bell, he waited anxiously for a response from within.

An eternity seemed to pass before a small slider opened halfway up the door, and an accusing eye peered out.

"Who dat!"

Although it was the opposite of how he felt inside, Svelt tried to act like nothing had happened. He didn't want Mrs Brown to suspect anything.

"It's me, Ol' Mama... Svelt."

"Svelt? Who dat?"

Old Mother Brown was a stickler for routine, and this was just part of the game.

"Mrs Brown. I have stayed at your establishment countless times over the last five years. Svelt. Small guy? Rocky complexion? Weirdest breakfast requests ever?"

"Oh, *dat* Svelt. Why didn't you say so? You can't be too careful, you know-ah. Bless my soul. Come rest your bones, an' I'll fix you up a snack-ah. It's a bit late... I was just about to lock up de place-ah."*

"Sorry, Mrs B, I just want to get to bed. It's been a strange day."

"Course, me dear. Your room is a-waitin'-ah."

"Ol' Mama, you are an angel."

"You jus' get your little ass to bed, young man! If I was an angel, I would be welcomin' folk in, not locking dem out-ah!"

He smiled, took the key from her, and walked along the narrow corridor to the end of the building, passing several doors along the way. A left turn and the entrance to his room stood before him, with the dining area opposite. Although the building boasted three levels, Mrs B thought it best to put him on the ground floor due to his unusual build, thus becoming *his* room ever since. It was simply a question of balance. The guests, all with a part to play, were like weights, cogs, and springs in a gigantic cuckoo clock.

Svelt turned the key in the lock for Mrs Brown's sake, knowing the frame had lost the willpower to retain anything metallic long ago. There was never any need for bags or luggage, as a troll usually had everything required for survival about its body. In fact, apart from the tunic he wore, all he ever carried was a leather belt and pouch to hold his money. He flopped wearily onto the bed, which consisted of a solid wooden base with a layer of feather-stuffed sacks spread out on top. The 'mattress' was a nice touch on Mrs B's part, but in Svelt's case, it was equivalent to sleeping on a leaf. Reaching for the tiny candle sitting by the bedside, the troubled troll pinched out the dancing flame. He lay in the dark without realising for just how long, running through the evening's events before drifting into uneasy dreams.

*The inn could not have been more 'locked up' if it was in prison. Mrs Brown's take on security involved wooden

planks and six-inch nails. The surrounding walls could be pushed over with minimal effort, but the entrance was going nowhere.

Breakfast Serial

Pry-minister, Victor The Fourth, awoke in his majestic four-poster bed. *Another day,* he thought to himself. *I wish I didn't have to do this.*

The Pry-minister of Landos wasn't voted in, not even by the committee. Instead, he and his male forbears inherited the privilege of ruling the city simply because they had been born. He felt his birth had been in the wrong place and at the wrong time. Victor didn't want to make decisions, didn't really understand politics, and wished he could go down to the tavern for a quiet beer every so often. The notion of faking his own death had crossed his mind, but like everything else, he would probably have to ask the deputy pry-minister to arrange that too… because he would only mess it up. In civilised lands everywhere, it is disturbingly common for deputy pry-ministers, secretaries-in-a-state, and other ministers and advisers to be more intelligent and politically aware than the chosen ones themselves. It had been suggested that a wild monkey could fill the role quite adequately, with the added advantage of being able to peel its own bananas.

A knock on the door shook him from his thoughts. As if on cue, the deputy pry-minister entered, his heavy footsteps echoing as he crossed the marble-tiled floor.

"Morning, sir. Sorry to bother you so early."

"Morning, Brutus."

"We had some rather unfortunate events last night."

"Really," yawned Victor. "What happened?"

"Murder. In fact, double murder! You will need to issue a statement, sir."

"Why? Murder isn't that uncommon in this putrid hell—"

Brutus waggled his finger. "Uh-uh, pry-minister."

"Sorry."

"*Because, sir,* this is *your* city, and such barbaric behaviour will never be tolerated while you draw breath... may the lord strike you down!"

"Really?"

"Oh yes, sir. And I wholeheartedly support your visionary designs for the future of this city, while applauding your undeniable bravery in the face of utter hostility."

"Right. Thank you, Brutus."

"Not at all, sir. The quill awaits."

By 'issue', of course, Brutus was referring to a required signature.

"Okay, I'm getting up."

"See you in the meeting room, sir."

The enormous troll stomped away.

*****

Svelt woke with a start. The simple room was devoid of natural light, which suited a character of his unique makeup right down to his path-worn soles. Even though he was of mixed species, both parents were of cave-dwelling lineage. He guessed it was almost breakfast time due to the various aromas drifting around the short space leading to the dining room.

"Mornin', dear."

"Good morning, Mrs B. Thank you."

Already on the table was a small bowl of aggregate. Gravel was great for the digestive system, especially when accompanied by a large mug of something similar to ultra-strong black coffee but more akin to tar. After his 'cereal', the offerings took on decidedly human tones, with cold meats on the bone and cheese aplenty to satisfy the dwarvish side of his appetite.

Once breakfast was over, Mrs Brown noticed that Svelt appeared troubled by something.

"Is everytin' okay, Svelt? You don't seem your usual self-ah."

"Yes, I'm fine, Mrs B, but I may not be staying again tonight. Can I pay my bill now? Y'know, just in case."

"Of course, me dear," Mrs B replied, slightly concerned. "Two sense, please, as always-ah."

After handing her the key and coins, he headed for the front door, which, he was pleased to find, had been temporarily relieved of marauder-thwarting barricades. Svelt had yet to see one but knew they were called 'Dem'.

"Thanks, Mrs B. You know, you are like another mum to me."

"You are always welcome, Svelt. Nex' time though, don't try to catch me out with de name, yes? You jus' be careful-ah."

Svelt shrugged, smiled, and gently closed the door behind him.

As he got closer to the city, it was a very different scene along the walkways and roads. Daytime brought forth all manner of activity as farmers carried their produce atop carts, and shop owners placed displays of various wares on tables outside. Devious others then tried to lighten said showcases—bypassing the quaint old tradition of paying—only to find everything nailed firmly to the tables, which, in turn, were chained to the wall.

Arlam Amstad, native of Sumacia and purveyor of mystical, magical... mostly useless artefacts, added the final touches to his bustling shopfront by placing a few ornate oil lamps here and there. Passers-by nodded or wished him 'Mornin'' despite the creepy... nay, *terrifying* mask he wore. More surprisingly, nobody gave a second thought to how a shop bursting at the seams had suddenly appeared on a corner—joining a row of more established buildings—overnight. People are like that. Particularly Angless people.

Spotting a few steps beneath a stone statue, Svelt sat before carefully pulling the map from his pouch to study it.

Flora and Flounder

They say beauty lies in the eye of the beholder. Among her own people, she may well have seemed plain and unnoticeable. However, to almost all other species, Vaessa Inajoor was stunningly beautiful. Crystal clear sapphire eyes, perfect, almost white skin, complemented by long silvery hair marbled with strands of blue. It is often said: if a female can wear a potato sack and ooze elegance, she is indeed a lady. In Vaessa's case, it wouldn't matter if it was still half full.

It didn't stop her from feeling all alone in the world.

Not because she was unique—there were many like her. Nor because she didn't have any friends... she had friends. She felt alone because she was the only elf in the city. Her people were the tree-dwelling folk of the great forests some two hundred and fifty miles north, Merewood and Knottswood. Different clans, but still very much *elves*.

The elven race would never stray from their own kind, as they were far too proud, even arrogant, in the opinion of some; nonetheless, her parents *were* of mixed heritage. She was born of an affair between a noble-elf and a humble elf maiden of Merewood. A fact not even hidden by name, as in Elvish, her titles were glaringly mismatched. Despite the awkward situation, she had not been banished or driven away, even though the irregular union was severely frowned upon—elves do not abandon their own. It was her own choice to leave. There was no denying the simplistic beauty of the life her elvish kin offered, but she had always felt a need for more.

She now worked at a flower shop in an affluent city area known as *The Squares*. She couldn't afford to live there, but she loved the place, and it was the perfect job for her as she mirrored the beauty and elegance of the delicate items she sold. The very reason Ms Flora had given her the job in the first place. She had noticed it instantly. Poise and an almost regal presence that, unbelievably, many others failed to see. In her artistic eyes, it was as distinctive as a single bluebell standing upright above the forest undergrowth.

"How are you doing, darling?" called Ms Flora from the back of the shop.

"I'm fine, Fiona."

Vaessa was carefully arranging a colourful display in the magnificent bay window.

"Are you going out tonight, dear? Surely there must be a handsome young man on the horizon now?" Fiona asked in a motherly way.

"No, Fiona. Not yet." The reply was that of bored resignation. As if this conversation took place on a daily basis.

"Tell you what…"

Here it comes.

"… tomorrow night, why don't you come to the vine bar with me? You get to meet some very nice people there… it's my treat!"

Nice people? What she actually means is rich men.

"Why not, Fiona? Thanks, I will."

"Wonderful, *wonderful*. And don't you worry, I shall arrange for a licensed Hacknee cab to pick you up and take you home. You can't be too careful, especially where you live."

*****

Staring at a near featureless object endlessly does not animate it or encourage clues to appear. Nor does flipping it over and back again countless times, but it's always worth another try.

A sudden commotion near the fruit stalls provided Svelt with a welcome distraction.

"Oi! Come back, you little thief!"

A young lad had scooped up a handful of nuts, stuffed them in his pockets, and was now tearing off down the road with his spoils. Unfortunately for him, his trousers had seen better days—especially the 'pockets'—and the swag was bouncing spectacularly along the cobblestones in random directions. Two transfixed observers sitting on a bench followed the entertainment with great amusement—if not a little age-related envy.

"Hah! Little rascal. Reminds me of meself at that age. Shame he dropped the nuts, though."

"Huh! Kids today," moaned the other man, "got no pence whatsoever!"*

In parallel, mirror, and multi-dimensional worlds, strange quirks of language caused by microscopic, evolutionary, and genetic variances are almost inevitable. One man's meet, for example, could quite easily be another man's poisson.

Librum, thought Svelt, concentration returning after the brief show. *I know how to get there, but what am I looking for? A marker? Another clue? Where do I start? What should I ask for? Presumably, a book, but then I think I may be a bit spoilt for choice in that department! I must trust the old wizard's words and be confident in my instincts to point the way.*

"Yes, of course," he reassured himself, "I'll know what to do when I get there, won't I? I'll work it out. It will be obvious. Stick out like a sore thumb. Nothing to worry about."

Wandering aimlessly around cathedral-like buildings for hours also doesn't flush clues—singing and dancing—from their hiding places. The librarian was agitated and flashed several well-timed glares in the hapless troll's direction.

"Once again, sir, can I help?"

"Er, just looking, thanks."

"Sir, I have a profound knowledge of these books and the accompanying filing system. If you would just give me a title? An author? A blindfold and PIN!" He brushed himself down and regained his composure. "My apologies. However, I must ask that, if I cannot be of assistance, you should perhaps leave, gather your thoughts and visit again… *when* you know what it is you are looking *for*!"

"You are probably right," admitted the frustrated troll. "I'll come back later."

"Please, take your time, sir. No rush."

Svelt nodded his thanks as he left the building.

The librarian opened a book and picked up an unnecessarily large stamp, which he brandished like a weapon. "I sometimes wonder if it is worth educating them at all."

A glass-vibrating *thud* made Svelt glance back to the library with momentary concern before he continued plodding along the road. Sitting on a bench in the bustling little area, he focused on the map again.

He died for nothing. They both did.

He wanted to tear up the useless piece of paper and throw it away, as anger and frustration almost got the upper hand. Calming himself, he decided to take a long walk through the backstreets heading for The Squares. Something was always going on there, and he hoped it would give his mind a break from the whole business. He glared at his hand and began to screw the paper into a ball. Releasing his grip allowed the map to spring back into shape. It wasn't magic— attention-seeking parchments (mainly demands and summons) simply object to being screwed up. At that moment, something grabbed his heart, and he knew he could never allow the marker to come to any harm. It would be like killing the wizard himself. He straightened it and put it back into his pouch. As he headed off again, the giant bell of *Tiny Tone*, the city's famous clock tower, rang out. It sounded twelve times.

Svelt moved warily along the narrow side streets. A lack of shops or anything of interest made his chosen route to The Squares slightly dull, but he felt it best given the circumstances. The only establishments along *these* oppressive walkways were the dark, dingy, uninviting bars that seemed to pop up too frequently for his liking. Unlike the taverns in the main areas, a gloomy aura surrounded them. He'd never ventured into one. Nor could he understand why the owners of these places allowed ladies to monitor the doors, considering the dangerous surroundings.

It wasn't long before music could be heard from somewhere ahead, instantly lifting the mood and the troll's spirit. As he neared, the noise level rose. Not only music but laughing and cheering.

Svelt emerged from what was jokingly known as Fleetfoot Street straight into the crowds of people. It was not high on the list of roads to be officially named by the committee, but the locals had taken it upon themselves—to mock the frequency with which certain undesirables were fleeing from somewhere *or someone*.

The Squares was a haven for vendors of every description, selling anything from local culinary delights to little 'earthenware' mementoes of Landos. Rats, carrots, and turnips were not exclusive to the city, but none of the other regions seemed to have embraced the idea of baking them in 'clay'. The tourism trade was probably a good few hundred years away for the artistically entrepreneurial merchants of the city, but, for now, most of the visitors (usually farmers or tradesmen from the north) couldn't leave quickly enough. They certainly did *not* want a miniature sculpture of Tiny Tone, made from what one hoped was clay, but most likely something more biologically natural. Many opportunities arose from the equine deposits left behind by visiting outsiders, and the cobbled streets were unexpectedly clean.

The current target market included the wealthy residents of The Squares and similar surrounding areas. Unsurprisingly, they *also* did not require a miniature sculpture of Tiny Tone—or *anything* involving the use of clay—but a goodwill gesture in the form of an anti-harassment tax usually did the trick for all concerned.

A colourful group of actors performing a play caught Svelt's eye as he tried to take everything in. They were using the steps of a grand building as a makeshift stage, which drew people helplessly towards the intriguing dramatics. He tried to pick up the thread of the story unfolding but was a little lost. At least there could be no doubting the identity of one of the characters, who wore a makeshift crown and a wooden board bearing his name glued to the back of his robe. Svelt allowed himself a nervous giggle, although, the significance of the little boy dressed as a monkey, peeling a banana for Victor's double, eluded him. To the side of the actors' stage, another showman stood, theatrically throwing shaped lumps of painted wood into the air—so *high* that his accomplice had time to dip into the pockets of spectators before they dropped back down.

After a while, he tore himself away from the play and sideshows and headed for The Inside Market. Before his first visit to this emporium of delights, he'd only encountered stalls of fruit and vegetables in the streets. The Inside Market was different. Some stallholders sold handmade jewellery and scents, while others proudly displayed paintings and poetry they had created. Wandering at ease, he stumbled upon a lady selling wooden charms and was instantly drawn to a beautifully carved couple holding hands. A baby in a basket soon followed, then a silver-coloured chain. Although slightly heavy, undoubtedly perfect for the intended recipient.

With the purchase complete, Svelt made his mind up and decided to go home. As much as he loved the atmosphere of Landos, this particular weekend had been quite different from previous visits. He looked around the main square.

I'll get some flowers for Mrs B and drop them off on the way to the bridge.

Somehow unnoticed on many previous occasions, it certainly stood out if you were looking for items of natural variety… Into-Flora! The shop boasted an impressive bay window showcasing a colourful display of blooms. He ventured over, opened the door, and a small bell rang above him.

"Good afternoon, sir," a soft voice welcomed him, "how can I help you?"

"Hello, I wou—" Svelt stopped mid-sentence as he looked up from the flowers. She was the most beautiful person he had ever seen.

"I'm sorry?" said Vaessa.

"—would like to buy some flowers," he continued blankly.

She laughed. "Well, sir, you've picked the right place."

"Svelt!" he blurted.

"I've not heard of th—"

"No… hah! That's my name… Svelt!"

"Oh, I see." She smiled, turning his craggy heart to lava. "Hello, Svelt, I'm Vaessa."

"What a beautiful name."

Oblivious to events while sitting in the back room, Ms Flora approached the counter and was visibly startled when she saw the small, stony figure standing in her shop. "Can I help you?" she asked without much conviction.

"It's okay, Fiona, I am looking after Mr Svelt," insisted Vaessa.

"Are you sure, dear?"

"Yes, you carry on. I'm fine here."

The shopkeeper spun around and disappeared into the back room again.

"Okay, Svelt. What kind of flowers are you looking for?"

The bashful troll felt a bit awkward. "Vaessa, did I say something wrong?"

"No, of course not. Ms Flora is a little old-fashioned, that's all. Please, take no notice. Right, flowers," she repeated.

"Yes, er... they're for Mrs B."

Vaessa shrugged. "Mrs B?"

"Oh yes, sorry, she is like a mother to me."

"Ah, how sweet. What about roses? We have red, white, yellow..."

Her enchanting voice floated around his head as he perused the shop dreamily. His eyes fixed upon something he had seen many times before but never fully appreciated. Until now. "There! I would like those, please."

Vaessa was slightly taken aback by his choice. "Yes... yes, they are beautiful, aren't they?" She walked over to the shelf, picked a bunch, and wrapped them carefully before handing the delicate bundle to Svelt. "Two sense, please."

All the while, Ms Flora had been watching through a small window. Svelt reached into his pouch and handed Vaessa a large, heavy coin.

The prickly proprietor couldn't contain her surprise. "A *round*!" she muttered under her breath. "Probably robbed somebody."

Vaessa handed him the change. "Thank you, Svelt. Goodbye."

"Goodbye... Vaessa."

Placing one hand on the door handle, he stopped and turned back. He took a single bluebell from the bunch and presented it to her. Before she could say anything, the door closed gently behind him. Ms Flora's eyes narrowed in distrust as Vaessa stared at the woodland flower in her hand. "How did he know?"

Svelt had several more emotions than the average troll—or dwarf, for that matter—but regardless of how they usually manifested themselves, 'in turmoil' was probably the best way to describe them as he stepped back into The Squares. He wanted to go home, but the wizard's face continued to haunt his mind, and now... Vaessa. He had just laid eyes on the most beautiful female he'd ever seen, and she even spoke to him!

The conflicting thoughts bouncing around in his head made his limbs temporarily useless. People in the street stared at him as he appeared to be arguing with himself while his legs steered him around in little circles. He almost *drifted* past a smart-looking tavern where people literally fell out of the door, *some* with a gentle persuader. 'Smart-looking' in Landos generally meant that doors, windows, and signage were still in place—blood and other bodily fluids removed almost daily.

"Hey! Nice flowers, pal! Lads, come and have a look at this!"

Howls of laughter followed.

"Didn't know you guys were the sensitive types! Hoohoo!"

The jeers and laughter snapped Svelt back into the real world. His initial anger turned to realisation when he glanced down at the delicate flowers in his fist, and a smile spread across his face. His current pose resembled a frieze crafted by a mason with an extremely warped sense of humour.

"Only joking. Come and have a drink with us, friend!"

Usually, he would have ignored the shouting and walked away, but so far, this city visit had been anything other than usual. With a shrug, he stepped into the lion's den.

"Do it again, Svelt!" roared the man, tears streaming down his face.

Ten scattered cocktail nails (brass) now decorated the table where Svelt and his new pal sat.

"No, no. Shhnot funny anymore. B'sides, I got thingsshh to do."

The Shiny Metal Feeding Receptacle was busier than The Trough (spirited hijinks were commonplace in the city too, but they could afford better signs) or any other tavern on the outskirts of Landos. It was also a lot louder and rowdier. Anyone brave enough to step inside couldn't help but get carried away with the atmosphere, which usually meant getting carried even further away in a cell cart.

Svelt desperately tried to focus, but nothing seemed to be working. He felt his body wasn't a part of him anymore, and everything happened in slow motion. The boys carried another tray of drinks over and sat around the table. He took the olive from the nail, ate it, and drained half of the beer from the mug.

"Go on then," said one of them, egging him on.

"Okay…" said Svelt, picking up two of the nails, "but thiissh isssh the larsst time!"

"Oi, shorty!" a voice bellowed from across the room. "You tink you own dis place?"

An enormous, angry-looking troll made his way menacingly over to the diminutive interloper.

"Nope! D'you shhink you own anyshhing?"

The smug grin on Svelt's face prompted his new friends to stop laughing and start edging away.

"WOT!"

If there *was* a troll-ish version of hell, it broke completely… and utterly… loose…

From Bar to Bars

Svelt struggled to open his eyes. His head felt like somebody was hitting it repeatedly with a hammer. Unfortunately, it wasn't the type connoisseurs use to tease a single square of toffee from the block—it was the type convicts use when they are chained together while trying to persuade boulders to become smaller. Slowly, his vision blurred into focus. He was relieved it came back at all. Svelt gradually realised he was staring at a stone ceiling. Turning over confirmed he was lying on a rusty metal slab, and there were steel bars set into a small opening of an otherwise solid wooden door. He instinctively reached down for his belt pouch... it wasn't there.

"He's awake, sarge. Do you want me to tell him?" asked the desk officer.

"No, Bert. The chief wants to speak to him."

The aching, bewildered troll sat in his cell and waited... and waited. Eventually, he had sobered up enough to walk to the door and shout through the bars. "Will somebody please tell me what's going on? Why am I here?"

After a while, the rattle of keys woke him again as the door was unlocked.

"Chief Lopez here to see you, troll."

A large man entered. The lapels on his shirt announced his importance. Svelt realised there was something different about him, as, size aside, he appeared human but didn't look like a local. He had cropped dark hair, brown eyes, and bronzed skin.

"Svelt, isn't it?"

"Yes, sir."

The chief sighed. "You're in a lot of trouble, Son."

"I don't even know what I have done wrong."

"What's the last thing you remember? Think carefully… this is important."

"I was in the library, I think. Yes, the library, that's right."

"The library?" replied the chief, somewhat surprised. "What were you doing there?"

"Er, I was looking for a city guide. To do a bit of exploring, take in the sights," he lied unconvincingly.

"Really? I've lived here most of my life, but I usually try to avoid looking at anything on my way to work. Perhaps you can enlighten me?"

"Er… well, there's Tiny Tone, and… and… the River Tame…"

"Please, don't hurt yourself trying any further. So… a clock tower, then. Famous because it is the only one in the city yet to have the bell nicked. And a river you couldn't put a small fire out with but *could* quite possibly walk across—no bridge required."

"Well, I *like* Landos, sir."

Inwardly, Chief Lopez was overawed by the little troll's sincerity—*he actually meant it!* "You obviously haven't spent enough time here, Son. Okay, let's leave that for a minute. Do you not recall visiting the tavern?"

"Tavern? Oh yes, vaguely, the… er… er…"

The chief rolled his eyes in resignation. "The Shiny Metal Feeding Receptacle?"

Just one, he thought to himself. *One sen for each time I've cited that damn place on a charge.* He also felt the unnecessarily long name was edging into his retirement before him.

"Yes, that's it! I do remember now—there was a fight. But everything after that is a blur."

"Think back further, Master Hamfist. Did you not also visit The Trough? Just outside the Bo area?"

It now seemed like such a long time ago, but he would never forget it. "Yes, I did stop there for one drink. Oh no! My bluebells!" he added as the memories started to return.

"What?" The chief shook his head. "Look, I'll make this easy. You were seen running away from the scene of a murder. The old gentleman with a pointy hat? Stabbed! Ring any bells? And let's *try* not to forget a second death in very peculiar circumstances, which you just happened to be right 'in the vicinity of' again!"

"It's true, somebody stabbed the wizard, and I tried to help him."

"Somebody? I'm assuming you can remember what this attacker looked like?"

Svelt's shoulders slumped. "No, he was too far away and fled when he saw me. I think he may have been wearing a cap."

"We have a witness, a very *trustworthy* witness. In fact, he is a priest—a holy man, no less."

"Chief Lopez, I think somebody is trying to kill me. I ran to help the wizard after he was attacked by another man— a man in robes. Yes, that's it… robes!"

"Not much to go on, Svelt."

"Please, you must believe me! The wizard said nobody could help him, so I panicked and ran. I ended up in that tavern."

"Ah yes, the tavern. Please continue."

"I was standing at the bar waiting for my drink, and the man beside me collapsed suddenly. Later, while collecting my thoughts, I realised I was the intended target. That poor man was simply in the way."

"Yes, nasty affair, tiny poison blow dart. Not the weapon *I* would use to kill a troll. Can you shed any light?"

"Sir, I have never used a weapon before— I don't even carry an axe!"

The chief realised Svelt was becoming a little hysterical, and pushing him further at this stage might not be beneficial. "Okay, Mr Hamfist, we'll leave it there for now. I'll have someone bring you a drink— not beer, I'm afraid, as Landos is a little short after your monumental quaffing efforts. Bert! Open up, please," he cried through the bars. Bert duly obliged, and, with utter dismay, Svelt heard the dreaded lock click again. "And get our new guest some water."

"Yes, sir."

Chief Lopez entered his office and sat at his desk, absentmindedly stroking the band of silver on his large forefinger. *Why? What's his motive? Money? No. He had very little when he was brought in, and there are wealthier areas to target than Bo.* After some deliberation, he quietly cursed himself and sat upright in his chair. "Frank! What's that guy's name?"

"*Guy*, sir?"

"The witness... the *statement*? You know, the priest... or is it preacher? Whatever he's supposed to be!"

"Oh, Zeqar, sir."

"Zeqar? Zeqar what?"

"Just Zeqar, sir."

"Just Zeqar, eh? Find him! And bring that shifty bastard in."

*****

"It's so unlike him," Jill said, fighting the tears.

"Just wait 'til he gets back! We've got two empty carts, a field full of bales to load, and we can barely lift one between three of us," Mr Barleyso raged. "Been at the grog again, I'll wager."

"No, Svelt's always been a good lad, never gets into any trouble; something's happened, something important has delayed him, is all."

"Sorry, dear," sighed Bill, realising his ranting was only upsetting his distraught wife further. "We're not due to take the dairy load into the smoke for two days yet, but I'll take a horse and go look for him."

"The city is huge, Bill. Just give him a few days, and he'll be back right as rain... I'm sure of it," she lied to herself.

*****

A mere three days as a guest at *The Booted Inn* (officially and unaffectionately known as The City Law Station) could ravage the unprepared soul in *unexpected* ways. No physical cruelty or torture took place, but any mind subjected to the inane questioning techniques of officers Dabble and Trubble, which invariably resulted in them interrogating each other, could start to lose grip of reason and reality. Add to that the menacing smiles of aspiring new recruit, Dirk Tombs, delivered with such ferocity that, in a duel, a supernova would blink first, and a man's spirit could be shattered with the similar effectiveness a dripping tap has on happy-go-lucky, non-suicidal types.

Fortunately, Svelt was not a man.

Dwarven spirit is legendary, and a *troll's* inner resolve could only be 'got at' with the repeated use of obscenely large hammers... usually *by* dwarves.

Unfortunately, he *was* a caring son.

I must let Mum and Dad know why I haven't returned home.

At first, he thought the chief would realise it was just a big misunderstanding and he'd be released, but there seemed to be no sign of that happening anytime soon. Nor had there been any change of mood towards him. He was a prisoner.

If they do think I killed those poor men, what now?

His mind went into overdrive, but it was soon snapped back to attention by the sound of keys rattling in the lock.

"Chief wants to see you."

In most instances, leaving a troll unrestrained—even in the confinement of a cell—would be considered unwise at best, especially one expecting to be charged with murder, possibly weighing up the last chance of escape. It was at the chief's request for reasons of his own. He was not led to the interrogation room, which surprised him, but straight to Lopez's office instead.

"Come in, Mr Hamfist."

Svelt noticed a slight change in the man's voice. No longer stern or questioning, more... borderline sympathetic. He hoped, against all the odds, it wasn't a regretful prelude to what the chief was about to say next.

"I see my officers have forgotten to apply the shackles. My safety is clearly of paramount importance to them."

"I'm sorry?"

"Were you not surprised to be left unrestrained?"

"I... no, it never crossed my mind."

"I would offer you a chair, but... unfortunately, we don't seem to have anything suitable."

"I'm fine, sir."

"Svelt..." he paused on the name, "you are in luck, my boy!"

Lopez *almost* broke into a smile.

The troll's heart lifted.

"A young lady came to see us earlier today, a *young lady* you probably owe your life to."

"W-what?"

"She says she saw the whole thing, Son. The wizard struggling with his attacker and someone fitting your description, 'nuff said, coming to the rescue. You are off the hook."

The young lady *had* identified Svelt while he slept in his cell, but Lopez didn't tell *him* that. Inside, the chief was congratulating his instincts *and* calculating possible outcomes.

"Thank you, sir. Thank you."

"*Please...* it wasn't my doing, Mr Hamfist. Thank your lucky charms that *this* witness was not as virtuous as our first." Svelt didn't understand the meaning, but at that moment, sheer relief negated the need for trivial details. "You are free to go, sir," added Lopez.

"But what about the real killer?"

"*Real*? Are you suggesting there are others with the capability who lack the intent?" The indecision inching across Svelt's face prompted a *slightly sinister* laugh. "No need for a reply. To answer your question... I let him go." This was met with another puzzled look. "But rest assured, he will not be so lucky the next time we meet. And we shall."

"What happens now, sir?"

"Go to the front desk and collect your belong—bits and pieces."

"Yes, sir."

"Before you go..." Lopez stroked the silver ring on his forefinger again. Svelt hadn't noticed it before, but now he was aware of unusual engravings which were difficult to make out.

Looks like an eye... "Yes, sir?"

"...we found a strange drawing amongst your items. Are you the budding artist?"

He felt inwardly relieved to learn that his pouch was still intact.

Lopez looked at him intensely.

Most trolls are blessed with an ability to control giveaway body language—something to do with a lack of pliable muscles—another troll, however, would have noticed the merest twitch of stone. As would a weather-worn, battle-hardened chief of the law.

"Yes, sir. I drew a little map of the area when I visited the library."

"Ah yes, of course… I remember now. You know, Svelt, *technically*, the murder in the tavern still hasn't been cleared up, so please stay out of trouble."

"Yes, sir."

"And the best way to do that, of course, is to *go home*."

"I will. Goodbye, sir."

Svelt needed no further encouragement and hastily left the room.

Lopez leaned back in his chair and stared at the closed door.

And when you return, Master Hamfist, which you inevitably will, we shall find our man.

Svelt was handed a piece of paper by the desk officer.

1 LARJ LEVVA BELT
1 LEVVA POWCH
1 ~~WERFLISS~~ METAL CHAIN WIV WOOD BITS
CORECKSHUN:^ PRICELISS AND DULY RETURNED
ONE STOOPID MAP
10 SENSE

"Ten sense!"* cried Svelt in dismay.

"Many things can happen when you get drunk in Landos, sir—*things* forgotten in the alcoholic haze."

"But—"

"In fact, I'd say you are lucky to be reunited with that expensive bit of jewellery."

Bert passed the items over with a knowing glare.

*Wandering the city with a pouchful of money is not advisable. Apart from the numerous opportunists only too willing to lighten the load, there is also the inevitable

incarceration to consider. City Law Station 'rools' state: Ten sense is the specified amount to ensure that a released person may enjoy a meal, drink, stay at an inn and have sufficient cab money left to vacate the immediate vicinity and sod off! This proposal was put forward by officers Fred Dabble, Benjamin 'Barny' Trubble, and—because he was conveniently placed— desk officer Bert Bungle. Just who it was suggested to is a mystery. Therefore, how it ever became a rool is a greater one. Obviously, if you came into the station with nothing, rest assured that you would leave unburdened with that exact amount. The station happened to be in a wealthy part of the city, but that was merely a coincidence. The one exception to The Ten Sense Rool only comes into force if a detainee's stay evolves into months rather than days, and they are transferred to a more secure facility. In this instance, the prisoner's notable effects are filed under 'came in wiv nuffin''.

Opening the pouch, Svelt poked the meagre coinage ruefully. "Yes, seems about right," he murmured, considering his narrow escape.

"If you would just sign here, Mr Hamfist," smiled Bert. The desk officer was not the best with letters and words, and he stared at the signature handed back to him as though it were a foreign language. As a scribbled 'X' was usually the order of things, Bert felt he should be quietly surprised and impressed by the erratically joined handwriting—even if he didn't know why. "Goodbye, sir."

"Bye."

Svelt walked out into the free air.

Building Bridges

"Vaessa. Va-es-sa."

"Oh, sorry, Fiona, I was daydreaming," Vaessa admitted as she placed a few roses into a gift box.

"Are you okay, darling? You're not ill, are you?"

"No, I'm fine… really."

"You didn't seem your usual bubbly self at the vine bar the other night. That nice young man offered to buy a drink, and you were slightly rude! Most, most, unlike you, dear."

"I didn't mean to be, I— he wasn't my type anyway."

"Really, darling? And what *is* your type?" Fiona asked sternly.

That's a good question. What is my type? An elf? No, I didn't want that life. Somebody like me? Yes, like me, but not *alike.* Vaessa sighed and glanced at the door. *I wonder if he'll come in today.*

*****

After deciding to get a cab out of the city, at least as far as the toll bridge, Svelt hoped to hitch a lift closer to the farm. He loved the sights, sounds, and even the smells of Landos, but right now, all he wanted was home. He was also thankful the map was safe, fearing he'd lost it forever after his arrest. It seemed to somehow invite danger, but he was glad nevertheless. He had considered showing it to somebody more knowledgeable than himself—one particular friend an obvious candidate—but then thought better of it. As the closed carriage trundled through the streets, a thought niggled at him. It wasn't the first time.

Should I have gone back to the shop?

He desperately wanted to see her beautiful face again but knew his mother would be worried sick by now. Watching the buildings roll by, a small wave of regret washed over him concerning Old Mother Brown.

I will make it up to her next month... with a big bunch of flowers.

A jarring bump and the audible change of surface beneath the wheels woke the snoozing troll as they left the city behind. They were approaching the Bo area.

This is where it all started. If I'd left Mr Singe's ten minutes earlier or not looked to the left at that moment, I would never have found it.

The reassuringly familiar sight of his favourite kurry house was the tonic he craved before entering open lands, and eagerly he waited for it to come into view. Don McCon's 'meatery' lay just ahead. The garishly colourful sign loudly announcing The Banal Spice hung in the background, swaying very gently. Still moving slowly, they pulled level with *The Home of Buggers*, and Svelt tried to peer in, but the light reflecting on the glass blanked out the inside. Just as they were nearing the bend, he noticed a woman walking into the building, and then... it was out of sight. The cab trundled towards the outskirts and headed for the river.

Thirty seconds later, a piercing scream filled the air, followed by the woman bursting back out again. Don called to her, but she was already well into her stride halfway along the road, with no intention of looking back. He re-entered the shop, shaking his head—the place was empty. *If* you ignored the tall figure sitting at a table with the pale, bony face. And a horse. *Technically*. The pile of bones artistically crafted into a horse shape stood perfectly still and stared out of the shop window into the street.

Technically stared.

The seated figure wore a black cape with a hood, partially concealing his skeletal features. A large tray of buggers sat on the table alongside a pile of money.

"Keep 'em coming, Big M," said the caped apparition. "More... more!"

"Ye must be starvin'," said Don, in disbelief, "or drunk!"

The figure paused momentarily, gently placing two buggers back on the table, and slowly lifted his head. A look of inquisitive surprise fought against 'features' unaltered for centuries.

"*No*, I'm *Famine**. I don't think I know Drunk, but *Starvin* is tall, dark, skinny, pushes a pathetic old carcass of an animal around, and has an insatiable kurry addiction. He's nothing like *me*."

An ancient, bony finger extended towards the door.

"Eh?" Don walked cautiously to a corner—a respectful distance from Famine's statuesque mount—and peered across to The Banal Spice. He smiled and politely returned the gesture to the hooded, ghostly face waving at him from a window opposite. Outside the Garamanian eatery, the oldest, most disease-ridden ox that *even Don* had ever seen lay in a dilapidated wooden hand cart, waiting patiently for its driver. Putting aside his mild state of shock, Don returned to the table.

"Ma apologies, sir. A case of mistaken... er... *identity*? Now then, will ye be wantin' potato with them?"

*The Horsemen, of which there are many more than the assumed four (some surprisingly mundane and not at all apocalyptic), are apparitions not usually visible to humans. Unless they are indulging, fleetingly, in physical activities—as opposed to ghostly, work-related tasks invariably resulting in the serious ruining of someone's day. There is no mention, for example, in any religious books of the dark rider who meticulously places a fly in bowls of soup throughout the universes. Which is why he gets the ass.

Svelt paid the fare and headed for the bridge while the driver turned the horses smartly before starting back. Halfway across, the eager troll lay in wait, sitting on what appeared to be a cut-down oak log. His massive hands were resting on a table made of solid wood, and nailed to the bridge posts behind him was a crude canopy covered with animal skin. He wore a large pouch around his waist secured by a rope. As Svelt got closer, he realised it was full of coins.

"Stop, mist— hey, it you!" said the troll, recognising him.

"Hello again, Ton. Well, look at *you*... what's this?" Svelt asked, pointing to the canopy.

"Boss say, it to keep off de elem— emen— lemon-ants..."

—casual dusting off of Svelt's tunic and exaggerated belt-tightening filled the void between words forming—

"de wevva!" exclaimed Ton triumphantly, with a black flint, stony smile.

"Well, you sure are doing okay for yourself now, eh pal?"

"Ha, yeah..." said Ton, leaning back with his arms behind his head, "boss say, if I keep it up—" there was a loud *crack* as Ton, complete with canopy, disappeared backwards over the edge of the bridge. "—I can go on ollydaaaaaay!" The impact caused an almighty splash, and a tidal wave of displaced water raced away in opposite directions.* For a split second, Ton was sitting on a muddy island. "Oh no, I really done it dis—"

He disappeared under a surge of water.

"Ton!" shouted Svelt, with genuine concern. He ran to the handrail, desperately looking for any sign of life under the turbid water, knowing the less-than-buoyant troll couldn't possibly float or swim. After an agonising wait, ripples of bubbling water broke the surface a little way from the reed-lined edge. Ton slowly emerged, and, without breaking stride, he simply walked up the bank. "Ton!"

"I okay, mister."

The currently misplaced bridge troll squeezed the considerably lighter pouch tentatively and whimpered. "Oh no."

With a sigh of relief and, realising it would take a while for his return, Svelt reached into his own near-empty pouch. "Two sense on the table, friend. It's a start!"

The dripping bulk looked across to him and waved. "Tanks, mister."

As Svelt turned to continue crossing the bridge, he was almost flattened by a galloping horse pulling a cart. The farmer driving returned the coin to his pocket, cracked the reins again, and smiled in blissful disbelief at his good fortune. Once clear, he looked back to the bridge and blew a raspberry. Ton slowly headed towards his table, a picture of pure deflation. His craggy face suddenly broke out into a rocky grin, and he blew a louder, longer raspberry at the long-departed farmer, gratefully scooping up the large cheese rounds dislodged by the sudden shift in speed.

A short while later, in the centre of Landos just past The Bridge Tower, a determined man in an old rowing boat struggled bravely against the 'water', transporting a modest cargo of exotic fruit to West Garamania Dock. A mountainous surge from both directions launched him a hundred feet into the air—he was above the boat, and the fruit was above him. During the short time he found himself liberated from the constraints of gravity, the bewildered sailor, oar still in hand, couldn't help but admire the fantastic view. Not long afterwards, the many varied species of 'marine' life in the River Tame were enjoying a delicacy that would not be invented for hundreds of years. A meat and fruit smoothie.

After a slow, uncomfortable journey inflicted marked deterioration to yet another cart seat, Svelt was relieved to enter familiar surroundings. "Thank you, sir," he said to the farmer while climbing down from the cart.

"You're welcome. Now I knows you're a coun'ry boy an' not a smoker, *Welt*, I promise I won't try an' run yeh over nex' time." He winked and nudged the horse into motion.

Svelt watched the cart trundle away, then set off down the narrow track marking the final stretch. He reflected on the events of his city visit, barely believing them himself. He had quite a story to tell. *If* he chose to.

A short while later, he rounded a long bend and stopped to take in the full significance of the sign.

He was home.

Jill Barleyso stared vacantly from the kitchen window as she washed the dishes. A task repeated unnecessarily many times since Svelt had failed to come home. Gazing longingly at the pathway which led to the front gate, she pictured her son striding up and opening it. She looked down at the plate she had been cleaning absentmindedly for quite some time. Shaking herself from her thoughts, she put the plate aside and glanced up again. Their son was strolling towards the house. Her hand automatically picked the next crockery item.

Our son is walking up the path!

"Svelt!" she cried, "Bill! It's Svelt!"

The plate smashed on the tiled floor as she ran to greet him.

*****

Two weeks passed on the farmstead, and it was as though nothing had happened. Svelt worked happily in the fields and carried out his daily duties as he'd always done. However, *initially*, there was the tricky affair of explaining why he was late coming home.

"A girl?" Jill cried ecstatically.

"Yes, Mum. I met a girl."

Although Bill had put his anger aside through sheer relief at his son's safe return, he still wasn't quite as enthusiastic as his wife. But it did give him a rare opportunity to pass on his worldly experience. "Got to be careful there, Son."

"Tell me all about her," his mother insisted, barely able to contain her excitement.

Svelt explained how he had met Vaessa, bending the truth just a little with his account of how they had become friends. Failing spectacularly, he also used his limited descriptive powers to relay how beautiful she was. Neatly glossing over the wizard, the map, *and* his brief stint in jail.

Almost three weeks had passed since his return from the city, and another working day in the field unfolded without complication or drama.

"Svelt! Dinner!"

The cry was music to his ears. He walked into a barn, yanked the handle on the water pump, and let the cool liquid run over his hands.

Food aside, family mealtimes had become a little strained, as he was petrified of letting something slip during general conversations at the table. It did not go unnoticed by his parents.

It was late evening, and following another hearty dinner, Svelt retired. A simple little room, very similar to his accommodation at Old Mother Brown's, the only difference being the view from his *window*, which was beyond priceless. As he lay on his wooden slab, the charm bracelet suddenly sprang to the forefront of memories regarding the recent trip. The gift intended for his mother had completely slipped his mind. He leaned over to the belt pouch hanging from the bedpost and emptied its contents onto the feather sacks. A few coins fell out, followed by the charm bracelet—the map landed gently after. Svelt stared at it.

The map!

Something that could not possibly slip from his mind, even though he'd tried. Seeing it again summoned old feelings inside, but he attempted to convince himself otherwise. "I have everything I need right here." He laid back. "Except Vaessa."

After a short, agonising while, he grasped for the map, but the sudden movement caused the small piece of paper to fly from the bed and float to the floor. He peered over the edge and stared at it, unable to break his gaze for what seemed like an age. Snapping himself back to the present, he left it on the floor and laid back again, but the recurring thoughts wouldn't allow him to relax.

The wizard died for it.

Once again, he fought against the guilt and regret in vain. Springing from the bed, he retrieved the piece of paper with some difficulty. The hazy evening light was still streaming through the window but sinking fast. He held the map up hopefully to the amber-coloured light, which dulled to red as he checked it over—the room was almost glowing. Several seconds later, Svelt staggered back onto his bed in awe at what the dying light revealed.

The previously unseen images on the map seemed to jump out at him, almost out of the paper itself! Where there had once been blank space now showed clearly visible streets and buildings. He didn't recognise any of them, as none were named. His head spun. Without really knowing where to begin, he instinctively turned to familiar ground.

LIBRUM.

It was the same outlined square as before, except now, tiny characters appeared within, including a clock face highlighting the number one. Two letters also occupied the square: S and T. He was so excited that his eyes wouldn't focus on any clue for long, but as quickly as the images appeared, they vanished as the last rays disappeared beneath the horizon.

That night, Svelt couldn't rest, let alone sleep. His head was filled with images that he didn't understand.

How can I tell Mum and Dad about this? Why is the night lasting so long?

Eventually, morning arrived. Jill Barleyso had never been happier, sitting at the breakfast table with the two people she cared for most.

Bill enthusiastically outlined the busy work schedule, but Svelt didn't hear a word of it.

"Mum, Dad, I need to go away for a while," he announced, finally plucking up courage.

"Weekend off next week, Son," Bill said brightly, slapping his son on the back but soon wishing he hadn't.

"No, Dad. I *mean*, I've got to go away *now*!"

Svelt said it with more authority this time, and his mother looked dismayed.

"But why, Svelt?"

"This is so hard for me to explain. *Please* trust me, and I'll be back as soon as possible."

Bill left the table in a huff. "Knew this was coming," he muttered, "it's her." He strode out of the kitchen, slamming the door behind him.

"Is it this girl, Son?" asked Jill.

He wanted to say yes, but he couldn't. "No, Mum. It's more important than that."

Mrs Barleyso looked at her son. "I understand… it's your natural parents. You want to find them, don't you?"

"No! No, Mum, you've got it all wrong, I promise. You are my true parents, and I don't think about them much anymore," Svelt reassured her. "Nobody knows where they went anyway. I couldn't find them even if I wanted to. I wish I could explain— I've got to do this."

Jill stroked his cheek and walked despondently to her bedroom.

Svelt stood at the front gate, preparing for the familiar journey, wondering if he was doing the right thing. In his heart, he knew he had no choice. The map would burn away at his very soul forever. Jill left the house to see her son off, and he met her halfway.

"Just promise me you will come back safely."

"I'll try, Mum," he smiled. Jill threw her arms around him, and he gently tried to do likewise. "Mum, I have something for you."

Reaching into his pouch, he pulled out the charm bracelet.

Jill looked at the three wooden figures behind floods of tears. "It's beautiful."

Opening the gate, he turned back and waved to her.

Mrs Barleyso watched her son disappear along the winding lane. She didn't know why, but it felt like a defining moment, and her heart said he may never return.

As Svelt left the farm and headed towards the carriageway, it wasn't long before the *clip-clop* of hooves closed in behind. He moved over to let the cart pass, but it stopped alongside.

"Well, what are you waiting for?"

He looked up, climbed onto the cart, and sat beside his father.

The greenery soon became sparse and scattered as they left the countryside further behind.

"Well? Are you going to tell me?" prompted Bill. He received a blank look in reply. "That bad, eh? Svelt, you're not in *real* trouble, are you?"

Svelt looked at his father's worried face and knew he couldn't hold it from him any longer. The words just poured out. He began with the wizard and map, ending hesitantly with his stay in prison. His father listened in amazement.

"But what is it that you're searching for?"

"I don't really know. The wizard said it was an artefact of some kind."

"If it wasn't for the fact that two people have already been killed, I would say it's quite exciting to have an explorer in the family."

"There is somebody out there, Dad, somebody who doesn't want it to be found at *any* cost, it seems."

"That is my only concern, Son. You're a tough lad, Svelt, no question of that, but you are no hunter *or* fighter."

Svelt knew his father was right, having never hurt a living creature or barely even argued with anyone his entire life. He did not feel afraid, though. If nothing else, the adventures of his last visit to Landos had at least made him aware of how dangerous the city could be.

"Dad, can we cut across to the south? I don't want to take my usual route. When we enter the city approach, you can drop me at First Bridge... next to The Tower."

"Where will you stay? Won't you be too far away from Mrs Brown's?"

"I have walked from the city centre to Hacknee many times before, but... no. My business starts in the centre, so I shall stay there. Anyway, I don't want to bring trouble to Mrs B's door."

"Okay, lad."

Bill pulled the horse to the left and cut across the eastern and southern routes, roughly following the River Tame. Although it was slow-going on the minor tracks, Svelt thought it worthwhile.

As they reached First Bridge, Bill slowed the cart and stopped—The Tower loomed imposingly to the side. Once an old guardhouse and checkpoint monitoring the comings and goings of the city, now used as a prison for particularly nasty crimes. It recorded a violent and bloody history. Hangings, beheadings, sacrifices, and battles were once commonplace within its stout walls, at least until what passed for 'civilisation' calmed things slightly.

"Thanks, Dad. Look, I—" Svelt began, but his father raised his hand to silence him.

"You don't have to explain any further, Son. Here, take this." He handed Svelt a leather bag heavy with coins. "I had thought about giving you a knife, but the only knife you've ever used is to spread butter!" he laughed.

Svelt hugged his father, emptied the coins into his belt pouch, and climbed down from the cart.

"Just try to come back in one piece, boy. If not for me, please, please, for your mother's sake."

Bill turned the horse around expertly and set off back towards the outskirts.

To-Toll Con-Troll

Com·mit·tee: *a selection of people appointed for a specific function by a larger group typically consisting of members of that group.*
Re·al·it·y: *a bunch of greedy, lazy, incompetent spongers who spend the money of others and are utterly non-representative of the people they supposedly serve.*

"Good afternoon, members. We are here today to discuss the possibility of introducing a toll," announced the chairwoman.

"Oh, that's nice. Where is he then?" asked an elderly gentleman holding a significant part of *The Landos Looters'* brass section* to his ear.

"Where's *who*?" replied the chairwoman. *Here we go again!*

"This troll you're going on about."

"Toll, Henry... TOLL!"

"Oh, that's his name too, is it? Could get a bit confusing, that," muttered Henry.

"No, that's *your* name! Hold on a minute..." she strode over to him and adjusted a small valve on the side of the horn, "... BETTER?"

"Alright, alright, bloody hell! I would've heard that from home!" he winced.

"Right, members, shall we start again?" As all that followed was incoherent mumbling, she decided on their behalf, which was nothing new. "Should we introduce a toll to First Bridge?"

"I don't know, bridges are quite fussy... d'ya think they'll get on?" said one member.

There was an explosion of laughter.

"Nice one!"

Cedric rolled his eyes and slowly shook his head in disapproval.

"If he's a typical example of the species, they've probably already met!" said another, slapping his thigh to prompt the reaction.

Another wave of laughing and cheering followed.

"*I* think we're better off without one A-TOLL!" Olaf chipped in, getting into the spirit and purposely glancing at Cedric.

Bellows of bellicose laughter followed, and one member almost died due to lack of oxygen. Over in the corner, Ronald was becoming increasingly frustrated with a coloured piece of chalk that refused to make a mark on his board. He threw it across the room, and it arced neatly into Henry's earpiece, rattling through the pipework. It was five minutes before poor Henry could focus again, and his eyes had stopped wobbling.

"Yeah, I'm all for charging a troll!" attempted another member, pulling a stupid face and holding his hands up almost in apology.

Cedric shot him a blank, menacing stare. 'Stony-faced' was already covered... naturally.

There was a short silence, followed by a hail of: "Boo!" "Shut up!" and "Rubbish!"

The chairwoman walked across the room as calmly as her internal boiler would allow, shaking her head while trying to avoid the array of missiles flying through the air. The hinges gave a pitiful creak as she closed the door gently behind her. The commotion from the meeting room could still be heard, even at the far end of the long corridor. She pulled her neat little jacket down to straighten it.

What am I doing here? I'm an engineer!

The unpolished brass section consisted entirely of Dave. The disharmonic orchestra began life as a trio, each with a different-sized loot, gradually adding various sections as they became more unpopular. The riots that inevitably followed were soon the main attraction.

*****

As Svelt crossed First Bridge, the shadow of The Tower cut diagonally away in the bright glare of daylight, much like an impromptu bundial. When his feet found stone again, he turned left, following the bank wall alongside the River Tame. He was excited but wary, too, with much to think about.

The distance to the general vicinity of the library prompted a steady pace. It was warm still, and using the bun's* position as a guide, Svelt took a rough guess at the time.

*Another minor quirk of language exclusive to Anglost, as was alluded to earlier.

"Spare a quart for an 'omless man, s— oh."

"Hello again, my friend," said Svelt, "I think I can spare another—"

"No... no need, sir. As I recall, *you* were more than generous."

"Are you sure?"

"Absolutely. I'm pleased to see yeh looking so... *sprightly*, sir."

"Er... yes. Thank you. Well, I'll be on my way."

"The *only* way now, sir. And well-deserved, too."

"I'm not sure I— the last time we met, there was trouble. *Wizard* trouble. Do you remember?"

"Can't say I do, sir, but that's wizard's for yeh. I take no notice, anyhow. Trouble... arguments... *fights*. None of my concern."

"No. No, of course not."

"Yeh can't change the path that has already been trodden. *My* concern is with the generosity of souls and to... *occasionally* guide the worthy."

"Right. And the best of luck to you... do you have a name?"

"Yeah, but it's a bit of a mouthful. Come from a very old family, see. Tell yeh what... yeh can call me Iris. Iris, er... Goode."

"*Iris. Goode.* May I offer you some advice, Iris?"

"Er... it depends. Get a lot of advice from the helpful citizens of Landos, y'see, and it usually involves nasty-sounding words I don't understand."

"That used to happen to me, too. No. I work in the fields in all types of weather, but the heat affects me most. It's a hot day, Iris... get yourself a hat."

"I will, sir! If fortune favours. Tread careful now... there may yet be a fork in the road for yeh somewhere ahead!"

"Thank you, Mr Goode!"

Nearing Westmines Bridge—still hugging the riverside—he noticed the discolouration of the water, which lacked the clarity of the outer regions where the troll bridges stood. As well as the general dark murk, there seemed to be a lot of debris floating around. He hadn't previously given it a second thought, but there was all manner of flotsam and jetsam building up along the bank. Making a mental note as he strolled by, he decided to write to the Council Committee suggesting a clean-up effort along the river. Based on past observations while leaving various taverns along the Tame, a new word for these intrusive elements sprang to mind—*pee-loose-on!* Another suggestion presented itself: *The Anti-Pee-loose-on Guard.* These brave souls would patrol the riverside and stop anyone attempting to throw rubbish—or evacuate various bodily fluids—into the River Tame, for which they'd surely be handsomely rewarded. Well, perhaps paid a wage deemed *almost* fair.

Forced to volunteer on the promise of a longer sentence if they refused?

Occupying his mind with this new idea, Svelt veered from the path beside the crawling, bubbling substance and headed into Westmines.

*****

Zeqar sat on an old wooden crate in an abandoned warehouse, reciting an ancient story from memory. No written words were required. Those who build chapters in recognition of their deeds need not thumb through the pages of books—this was an actual memory. Whether anybody else believed it or not was irrelevant because he knew it was the absolute truth. Many of the people he 'met' on his missions of mercy thought him to be completely mad, and belief is an individual right of choice, but none believed it for long. There are many ex-people who now firmly believe in 'deadly' instead. This description could also be levelled at Death, and accurately so, but in a way that was more a part of his natural makeup than anything he had control over. With Zeqar, it was different. He worked on it in his spare time, which was plentiful. In a way—the way of mysterious movement from above—it was *all* spare.

It niggled at his non-conscience that he couldn't be in his church to recite memories, but he was being hunted by the law, that much he knew. The law held no fear for *him*, but they were a nuisance—an interference to his objective—which he could do without. Someone was meddling with time, but even his lord would not use that precious commodity to aid their cause. At present, he wasn't sure of the precise whereabouts of his 'objective', and The Lord would not interfere at this point in proceedings.

It didn't matter.

"I shall be there at the end," he said quietly. Mercifully, the accompanying smile was only witnessed by an unfortunate rat, who would later be savaged by the pack… for its own good.

*****

Svelt crossed the busy road and entered the hustle and bustle of Westmines. Sitting on a thick log with shallow carved hollows for seats, he figured out what to do next. The air was filled with the noise of carts trundling along the cobbled street and snippets of conversation as people strolled by. Carefully, he took out the map, placed it on the seat next to him, and began to study it. Just one square was visible at the bottom, plus two little symbols on the side that had always been there—an eye and a triangle. He suddenly thought back to the ring Lopez wore and contemplated whether the chief could be complicit.

Holding the paper aloft allowed the light to animate it again. Svelt wondered why it showed so many buildings and if they all contained clues. If the drawing was a genuine map, then the areas depicted must exist and located near Old Town.

He lowered and raised it several times, convincing himself magic played no part. The other boxes representing buildings had always been there but remained invisible unless exposed to natural light. Unlike the heavy black outlines of the LIBRUM, they were the same colour as the paper and almost seemed to be *inside* it. He turned his attention to the clock image. It pointed to one, so he assumed that could only mean past-merid as the library wouldn't be open in the early hours, instantly dismissing the notion of breaking in.

S-T? The initials of a book title? An author, maybe? Or they refer to a particular section of the library. That will still lead me to the same search areas anyway.

A grimace surfaced in recollection of the sheer size and length of the aisles.

He put the map away with his mind made up. Tomorrow, at one, he would pay another visit to the library.

Checking in at *The Hard Rock Cave*, just outside the main Westmines area, brought a little comfort to his overworked mind. It was a specialist inn run *by* trolls, *for* trolls. If nothing else, Svelt knew it was the safest place to spend his evenings. Anyone stupid or brave enough to attack a troll in The Cave was almost certainly made of rock in at least two vital areas. One above the shoulders, the other below the belt.

After a quick scan of his room—no windows, wooden slab, and a candle lantern—he ventured to the bar. To a human ear, the noise was deafening. Trolls extending the customary greeting in their own language could easily shatter windows, so as you would expect, The Cave didn't have any. Native greetings aside, though they spoke in Angless (albeit a craggy form of the language), it was still horrendously loud.

Large flaming torches hung on walls of solid stone, probably considered slightly dangerous in more conventional taverns, but nothing remotely flammable could be found anywhere close by. No wooden furniture, nor any material covering the crude, roughly-hewn offerings, and curtains were obviously pointless. Even the drinks were not technically alcoholic—more tar-like than liquid—and sometimes they were lit purposely for effect anyway. However, that little indulgence was usually reserved for *Rocktale Night*. The acrid smoke and fumes were drawn out by vents in the walls, while the exterior was suitably plain without even a door at the entrance, just a steel gate, which could be locked if required. The landlord had a duty to protect innocent passers-by, on occasion, when things got even rowdier than usual. Given some trolls never sleep, the place had a distinct 'twenty-four/seven' feel.

The beautiful bar, which was nothing more than a colossal block of marble, had proven to be a *slight* problem. It was much higher than a standard tavern bar, as Svelt realised when he ordered a drink. Deep, rumbling, anonymous guffaws echoed from a hidden corner somewhere.

"Don't you worry, friend, I bring drink to you," said the helpful barman.

Svelt signalled gratefully. "Thanks."

A few minutes passed before the barman arrived at Svelt's table with all the grace and subtlety of a rhino on skates. "Sorry, pal, we got no olives."

Louder anonymous guffaws escaped from the other side of the room.

"No problem. Sorry, what's your name?" asked Svelt.

"Percy," replied the troll, this time to open laughter.

"Thanks, Percy. I'm Svelt, by the way… (expectant pause across the room) …Svelt Hamfist."

For a split second, the roof actually parted ways with the building.

"See wot I 'ave to put up wiv," moaned Percy, walking away.

After a brief sober spell of inner debate, Svelt downed his third drink and sprang to life. "Right, that's it! I'll be back soon," he said to Percy, walking towards the entrance.

"Okay, friend."

Svelt strutted purposefully in the direction of The Squares.

Vaessa was hard at work removing wilting flowers from their bunches and tidying the shop.

"Ready to lock up, darling?" Fiona called out.

"Almost." Vaessa swept the floor near the counter and moved towards the door—just as Svelt pushed it open. "Sve— sir, it's you. How are you?" she recovered, steadying herself. Inside, she was jumping for joy, and her heart was racing.

"Vaessa, I—"

"You remembered my name."

"Yes, of course. I could never forget it. Vaessa, this may seem crazy, but… may I take you out tomorrow night?"

I've done it! I've actually asked!

"Where would we go?"

Svelt hadn't thought this far ahead and started to panic, realising The Cave and various other troll-filled haunts were out of the question. "I… er…"

Vaessa came to his rescue. "I know a nice little vine bar just around the corner from here."

Svelt couldn't believe what he was hearing. "That sounds perfect. Is, er, seven okay?"

"Yes, meet me here, outside the shop."

He was so overcome that he couldn't say anything else. Instead, taking her hand as gently as a troll was able, he kissed it. Turning swiftly around, he barely managed to stop himself from walking *through* the door before opening it and leaving the shop.

Vaessa stood there with a radiant smile on her perfect face.

"Vaessa, what are you doing?" Fiona asked accusingly. "You are far too good for *him*… *that*… it!"

"*He* may be far too good for *me*, Fiona. Who knows? He is like me, alone and different, but we are not *alike*. In fact, he may just be my type."

Tombs and Tomes

Svelt had lots of new friends. Overwhelming joy and sheer disbelief prompted him to buy everyone in the bar a drink. Now, they all wanted to know him. "Tank's Svelt!" or "Wot you 'aving, Svelt?" It didn't get any better than this—a date with a beautiful girl *and* drinking with friends. *Real* friends!

Despite his euphoric state, a large shadow still loomed on the horizon. He slumped heavily onto a stool of stone, and the reality began to sink in again. "What are you doing?" he muttered to himself. Looking around hazily at the trolls guzzling drinks, shouting, and play-fighting reminded him of the night he was arrested. "Not this time. There's too much at stake."

Standing unsteadily, Svelt slipped quietly away and headed to his room.

*****

Unwilling eyes flickered open, and the panic of unfamiliarity washed over him before the memories and objectives returned. Today was the day. He couldn't wait for the evening to arrive, but first, a niggling annoyance required Svelt's attention. The distant echo of voices and general noise drifted up from the bar, but it was nowhere near as raucous as it had been the night before. There was no accurate way of telling the time when waking in a troll's room, but something dormant deep within the body just seemed to know. Unlike Mrs Brown's place, The Cave had no dining room or any set mealtimes. At various intervals, huge platters of meat on the bone, bread, cheese, and bowls of gravel—along with other trollish savouries—were unceremoniously dumped anywhere possible. In *this* establishment etiquette had gone right out of the win— small, smoke-syphoning vent! In truth, there was little evidence to suggest it had ever set foot in the place. In other hostelries, this complete free-for-all may have caused headaches when it came to billing the guests, but in The Cave, it was characteristically simple—a set amount was added to every bar bill for the food. Trolls always fought over it and tried to eat as much as possible at each 'sitting'—it was part of their upbringing. The landlord left it to them to make sure they each grabbed their ten pounds of flesh, and although trolls were not considered the smartest of creatures, they developed whole new levels of ingenuity to ensure they were first to get their quota. This ranged from simple yet cunning booby trap devices to plain, old-fashioned, extreme physical violence. It is widely believed the beloved circus clown evolved from mealtime shenanigans at The Cave, and the only additional ingredient required for the otherwise perfect slapstick routine was the custard.

After 'obtaining' at least some of his food allowance, Svelt exited into daylight. The sky seemed a little cloudier than it had been of late, but it still felt just as warm to him. He made his way to the Old Town in Westmines. The Old Town was generally believed to be the nucleus from which the city now spread. The area provided the first church, followed later by the inns and shops—in short, the buildings were among the oldest in Landos. Now also headquarters to various ruling authorities, including council and law. Indeed, the pry-minister himself resided there.

Although the first villages may have originated in Westmines, the rulers of Landos were loathe to admit they may not have been the first inhabitants. It wasn't until construction began in earnest that they discovered a vast new world *underground*. Unbeknown to many city natives, this was how the area of Westmines had acquired its name; the evidence suggested the dwarves probably got there first. Sadly, the hardy little folk currently adding to the city population were relative newcomers to the area, and even the oldest among them had no stories to tell of the endless tunnels and catacombs below the cobbled streets.

Svelt rested in the old square and looked at the library with a sense of foreboding. It was a beautiful building, but the tall entrance columns made it slightly imposing. To make things worse, he wasn't sure whether to enter the building at one or be inside *waiting* for the all-important moment. He assumed whoever had gone to so much trouble over the map would surely not be reliant on such trivial details.

Svelt entered the library as the bell struck one. Once inside, he felt extremely nervous, albeit a different kind of nerves to those he would undoubtedly experience later that evening. Walking to the front desk as calmly as his limbs would allow, he tapped his rocky palm on the smooth, wooden surface.

"Good afternoon, sir. How may I help you?"

The librarian was a small man with a pale, freckled face and wore seeing glassettes. He was smartly dressed, and despite the lack of hair on top of his head, he had enough on the sides to go around. Svelt stopped staring at him and sparked into life.

"Afternoon, my good man. I am looking for, er, S-T."

A bored, on-looking primate suddenly showed great interest.

The librarian, unsurprisingly, remembered the dwarf troll as soon as he'd walked in. Despite their last meeting, his greeting had been sufficiently polite while projecting helpfulness and professionalism. So, the current question agitating his seething mind was: *Why in the WORLD am I being asked for S-T?* He calmly exited the violently dangerous vault within his head, locking it firmly, and gave Svelt a most unconvincing smile. "Aren't we all, sir, but could you be *slightly* more specific?"

"Oh, yes, of course. Do you, by any chance, have a book…" began Svelt, testing the water. The librarian stared at him in disbelief, "… beginning with S-T?"

The little man drummed the desk with his fingers. "S *or* T?" he asked testily.

"Yes, please," beamed Svelt.

Something about the 'person' standing before him irritated the librarian immensely, but he decided to play the troll at his own game. "Please, follow me, sir." He led Svelt a long way from the entrance area, passing towering bookshelves flanking endless aisles, eventually stopping a few rows short of the end wall. "This row is S. And *this* row… is T!" he smiled triumphantly. Svelt looked along the row of S, unable to see the end. He could barely see the *top* of the bookshelf mountain. Feeling thoroughly dejected and somehow managing to look it too, he inadvertently cheered the librarian up beyond measure. "Please feel free to use the climbers *if* you so desire. You may take chosen books to one of the many reading tables at your disposal, but! Under NO circumstances can you take a book out of this library... understood?"

A nod of confirmation and Svelt was left to his own devices. The keeper of books clearly wasn't part of the ongoing puzzle as hoped.

High above, Shajar-wah was having grave doubts.

This cannot be right. It should be a wizard, an engineer, an inventor... or a man of science. Not a walking wall! Is this what I was summoned from Yu-at for! What shall I do? Should I change the next marker and end it there? Look at him!

He struggled with his conscience and then relented.

He has *come this far.*

Shajar-wah the Observant looked at Svelt's big, honest, innocent face and reached a decision.

Very well, then, a compromise. I shall let him proceed, but the next marker will be a test.

Descending rapidly and silently, he made a hasty adjustment at the bottom of the bookcase before climbing effortlessly back to the top.

"This is hopeless!" Svelt half-shouted, completing another pointless sweep of the aisle.

"Ahem!" reminded the librarian from the vicinity of the front desk.

"Sorry."

The impressive, leather-bound books were like a uniform army without faces to set them apart. They may have started with an 'S', but he could barely pronounce half of them. He decided to try the next aisle, hoping something would simply jump out and present itself. It didn't. Row upon row of almost identical-looking tomes stared back at him, the only difference being that the titles began with a 'T' instead. He walked to the end. Nothing.

"That's it," he said quietly, "I tried."

While setting off back down the same aisle to leave, Svelt sensed he was being watched, and at approximately halfway, something landed on the floor a few feet away with a *splat*! He almost jumped out of his stony skin with fright. It appeared to be an exotic fruit, purple and unlike anything on the market stalls in The Squares. Whatever it may be, he was sure it didn't belong in a library. Given the strict, quietly violent nature of the man in charge, Svelt knew it wouldn't be long before his finely tuned receptors detected something out of place. He peeped around the corner at the end of the aisle, where he was pleased to see the librarian busily stamping books… with slightly more force than necessary. Returning to the place of impact, the bemused troll looked up, wondering if a bird had carried it in. He kneeled for a closer look, and the discovery—albeit *slightly* prompted—was made! Shajah-wah rolled his eyes and picked a troublesome flea from his ear. The flea would have been proud to know it was, at that precise moment, the oldest insect on the planet*. Seconds later, a firm pinch ensured it was a posthumous title.

*Trillions of insects exist in the spirit world, but have you ever seen a flea's gravestone?

On the bottom shelf, wedged between two magnificent volumes, sat the thinnest book Svelt had ever seen—*if* indeed it was a book. He gently removed it. As light as a feather, very flimsy, and bending from side to side in his hands, it lacked any hard leather-bound cover to support it. The object consisted entirely of glossy pages, and he wasn't as quick to rule out magic on this occasion. A painting of a woman's face adorned the front. The colours were incredible, vibrant and almost alive! The woman seemed to be looking directly at him, and he thought she might speak at any moment. He studied the two big words at the top, which he assumed was the title, as the wafer-thin spine offered little room to write anything. The first word didn't make any sense—unless they were initials: TV. But the other, he was sure, spelt *Times*. He flicked through the smooth-feeling book in a state of awe. It held many more paintings, one of which made him pause for a second—a strange-looking carriage of unusual shape with spokeless wheels. He recognised most of the words, but the book's layout was unlike anything he'd ever read. Captivated by its beauty, the intrigued troll leafed through it several more times *until*... a single piece of paper fell from the pages and floated gently to the floor.

Svelt picked it up. Not only was it exactly the same size as the map, but seemed to be made from identical paper. The two ever-present symbols appeared inside the left border again, but the black library square was missing, leaving the page otherwise blank.

"Everything alright, sir?"

The call came from the librarian, who had silently appeared at the front end of the aisle. It startled Svelt, but he answered calmly.

"Yes, thank you. Almost done now."

"Very well, sir."

The cantankerous custodian returned to his desk, and Svelt breathed a sigh of relief as he was sure the librarian didn't know about the book he was holding. He turned it over several times, admiring it again, recalling the warning regarding books taken beyond the library threshold. But this was different. Looking around casually, he started to slide the book under his tunic. The hunched figure watching from above gave a disapproving screech of horror, which echoed around the library. Svelt heard voices in the next aisle and panicked—quickly removing the book again, he placed it back on the shelf. Shajar-wah was calm once more. Putting the paper in his pouch, hoping it was another marker, Svelt headed swiftly to the exit.

"Thank you very much."

He dropped a sen into the box on the librarian's counter.

"Why, thank you, sir. Most generous. I'm so glad we could finally be of assistance."

He smiled weakly at the dwarf troll, who tried his best to return the empty gesture before leaving the building. The librarian's inbuilt suspicion alarms were clanging with all their might.

Shajar-wah checked the immediate vicinity before swiftly descending the bookshelves to the ground below. He removed the book and put it into a bag on his shoulder. As he moved towards the climber, he stopped mid-action and shook his head. Turning back again, he reached down to scoop up the squashy remains of the dropped object and put that into the bag, too. An experienced case-hopping dimensional traveller, such as he, understood the dire—possibly exponential—consequences of such a rudimentary error.

He climbed back to the top of the bookcase and leapt across the aisle to the next. Rapidly covering the distance, the ancient baboon reached the back of the building and stood at the edge, staring at the solid stone wall a short jump away. It was quite a drop to the walkway below. He sniffed the air, waiting until he could *feel* the static. At precisely the right moment, he leapt into the rapidly thickening air and vanished over the library below… with a tiny flash of light.

Baring Wall

Searching for somewhere private to examine the second marker wasn't easy. Someone was always watching or listening in Landos, and although there was no shortage of dead-ends, dark corners and shady streets, they were tantamount to an admission of intent, which is *why* they were always empty. He intentionally avoided The Cave, fearing another heavy drinking session leading to a lack of concentration... or worse. Two more taverns sat opposite—temptation everywhere—but he decided they were out of bounds, too. Something was holding him back, an inner voice warning against studying the map further, something beyond explanation. While contemplating the various options, a thought suddenly struck him concerning Vaessa. Although he had until seven, he felt he needed a new look—something more appropriate for a vine bar.

Approximately thirty minutes later, Svelt hurried out of the de-finer clothing shop, trying to hide his embarrassment. "Very sorry, Mr Sarchy."

"Don't worry, Svelt darling. Try Doc's stall in the marketplace. I'm sure he will have something more suitable for your... *unique* build."

"Will do, Mr Sarchy. Thanks."

Mr Sarchy waved as the tiny troll slunk away, and creative cogs cranked into motion.

Time to think about the smaller— bigger picture. There is a huge— small market out there! After all, we are not living in the dark ages.
Owtsize!

Doc Taroo turned out to be a dwarf. Which had been a huge relief to his mother. A slightly nervous Svelt, undergoing substantially more than a once-over from said dwarf, reserved judgment at this point.

"So, Ver sent ye, did he?"

"Ver?"

"Aye, Vergenon. Vergenon Sarchy. A nicer fella ye'll not meet, and talented clothman too, but... a wee bit fancy for my liking, laddie, what with metal, gems, and tassels everywhere. If ye want plain an' simple, ye've come to the best place. Right! Bit taller and broader than yer average dwarf, hmmm... I reckon something hardwearing and on the loose side. Ye can't go far wrong with this, lad," he decided, pulling a shirt from a clothing rail.

"Wow! Thanks, Mr Taroo... I'll take it."

"Please, call me Doc," insisted the dwarf. "Surely ye'll be wanting to try it on, lad?"

"Er, okay. But where?"

Doc pointed. At the back of the covered stall, he had fashioned a 'changing room' by installing a rail with a curtain inside the rear canvas, creating a small space.

"Oh. Okay, great. Thanks, Doc."

Svelt took the shirt and drew the curtain. "It's a bit warm in here, Doc."

"Aye, that'll be on account of the lanterns, lad. You'll want to see what yer doing, right?"

"Sure... okay."

The resulting display resembled two boxers trying to fight inside a small sack. Meanwhile, on the *outside*, Mrs Liv Taroo was proffering a collection pot to a gathering of cheering female dwarves. A second, instantly removable sign hung on this side.

DOC TAROO'S TARDY
NEXT SHOW ~~12pm~~ ~~1pm~~ ~~2pm~~
DEPENDING ON CUSTOM

Most of the competing stallholders—particularly the proprietors of *Carroty Cakes*—had protested many times to the law about this sideshow. Officers Fred Dabble and Barny Trubble, who, unfortunately for the residents of this particular area, fell loosely under that heading, had assured them that Mr Taroo was paying a licence fee to them *personally*. To ensure it was all above board.

"Get 'em off!" screamed one of the ladies as Svelt's muscular, silhouetted figure fought against the confines to change shirts.

"What was that, Doc?" asked Svelt. "Thought I heard something."

"Ah, s'nothing, lad. Just the ladies at the cake-tasting stall over the square," he lied.

Svelt struggled to get his tunic off and bent over to pick up the new shirt.

"Shake 'em, baby!" another rather elderly lady shouted and had to be led away through exhaustion.

He managed to get the new shirt on to cries of: "Get 'em off again!" and eventually emerged from the changing room.

"Awwwww!"

He could have sworn a chorus of female voices moaned in unison.

"Well, Doc, what do you think?"

"Looks grand, lad… grand."

"How much do I owe you?"

"One sen, please. Er… don't ye want to change back into yer tunic?"

"No. I'll keep this on, thanks."

Mrs Taroo walked in. "Hello, dear," she said, smiling.

"Hello," replied Svelt. He handed Doc the money. "Hold on, Doc, I just want to check something." Svelt walked around to the back of the stall just in time to see a few dwarf women scuttle away. He also caught a brief glimpse of Mr Sarchy walking hurriedly in the opposite direction. He scanned the area, checking for anything unusual. *Just a plain canvas stall,* he thought, shrugging his shoulders. Returning to the front, he shook Doc's hand. "Thank you, sir, great shirt. You have saved my life."

Doc peered into the collection pot and smiled. "The feeling's mutual, lad!"

*****

As he reached The Cave, Svelt paused for a few seconds, bracing himself for the inevitable onslaught. Walking tentatively through the inn, it had started with *one* but quickly escalated into a crescendo of wolf whistles.

"Hey, Svelt! I know you *like* Percy, but dat shirt's a bit much."

A barrage of booming laughter hit the rafters, but the roof had learned its lesson and stuck to its job.

"Shut'cher gob, Rom!" came the retaliatory shout from behind the bar.

Svelt laughed along with them and smiled, easing his way awkwardly towards his room, tunic in hand.

"Come an' 'ave a drink, pal," called Rom.

"Can't today, guys. I'm meeting someone."

"Wheeey-heeey! Svelt got a boulder on de side!" Rom winked and elbowed Bam so hard that gravel shot out of his mouth like bullets.

"Hey!" Bam protested, shoving Rom and almost making him 'spill' some of his drink. Luckily, tar takes a while to detect sudden shifts in movement, which is just as well because a troll can take almost as long to react.

Trolls never pass up the opportunity of a good-old fist-fest, all in the name of fun, of course, so it didn't take long for the others to join in. One dejected troll was without a fight partner and could not get a foothold anywhere in the pile of thrashing bodies. Feeling left out, he sat at a table and smashed a large mug of liquid over his head. After all, he didn't want the others to think he was abnormal. Unfortunately for him, it turned out to be torch fuel, which was ignited by the flame as he stood again. The fighting stopped briefly, interrupted by screams that almost caused the wavering beams above to have a fleeting relapse, as the troll ran through the bar with his head on fire. Svelt watched from the doorway, shook his head, and left them all to it before escaping to his room.

He sat on his bed clutching the blank paper, confident it would reveal another location. Assuming consistency was the key, he held it to the candlelight and strained his eyes in expectation. Sure enough, very faint images were visible, but the flickering, dull light made it difficult to make them out. He needed natural light. Svelt hesitated again. It wasn't a feeling—more like a whispered warning in his head. Returning it to the pouch, he laid back.

There's always tomorrow.

*****

"You wanted to see me, Head."

"Yes, come in, come in. I'm sorry to say I've had word that Grindle didn't make it."

"Oh, bad show. When's he coming back?"

"No, Simson. He didn't *make* it."

"What! But… how…?"

"More to the point, *who*."

"A messenger?"

"Yes, I'm afraid so. And not just any old messenger, either. One of the first… one of the best."

"Poor old Grindle, he was a nice chap. Greedy bugger, but very nice chap."

A brandy glass toppled from Fezlet's table and shattered on the stone floor.

"Best not to speak ill of the dead. Bit cold in here, don't you think?"

"Yes, now that you come to—"

"We are all greedy buggers, Simson. *You* more so than most! Anyway, obviously, the map didn't reach our friend."

"The inventor?"

"He isn't held in that regard yet, I'd say, more of a tinkerer. And he's doing a damn fine job ensuring nobody would consider him as anything other."

"Yes, he is rather clever at disguising his true intellect."

"No, not really. Our young man is remarkably clumsy and inept, considering his endlessly creative mind. But you often find that to be the case when a genius, in theory, is charged with mundane tasks."

"Why *didn't* he make it as a wizard, Fezlet?"

"Far too intelligent, dear boy…"

"Yes, I see what— eh? Hang on a—"

"… but more importantly, not a single spark of magic in his whole body."

"Ah… that would certainly put a damper on it."

"Anyway, innocents are now involved."

"Oh dear, that is never good."

"It's worse than that. We already have a fatality, a mere bystander."

"Damn! Now wh—"

"*And* the map has been acquired by an unknown."

"Friend or foe?"

"Hard to tell at the moment, but our ancient primate friend is aware. Popped up quite unexpectedly in the old East Wing Library."

"I didn't think it was used anymore, full of ancient, outdated books."

"Tell that to old Rizzla. He nearly choked on his crafty mutton and carrot pie… poor chap."

"Oooh, nasty. Mutton can be a bit dodgy at the best of times, but *crafty*?"

"Precisely. Anyway, I somehow think the 'old library' angle is, in fact, the point."

"Yes, of course. How silly of me. Well, at least our furry friend knows… that's something."

"Any being capable of harnessing time the way he does is a force to be reckoned with. We may have no control over travellers putting in a sudden appearance from time to time, forgiving the pun, but I would never permit meddling from within these walls."

"Quite. Dangerous stuff, time."

"The Triangulans will always try to help us advance our slow-moving progress at a greater rate—they were a marvellous race. Snuffed out far too soon by their deity-worshipping kin."

"But why all the charades and shenanigans?"

"Because our friend is mischievous. A player. He likes to test us—make us prove our worth. Unfortunately, sometimes that can prove costly… to some poor blighter."

The desk candle sputtered fiercely before reigniting again.

Simson looked at Fezlet, who nodded slowly.

"So, what now? Do we intervene?"

"No, Simson. Magic will only draw attention and make things worse. Besides, officers of the law are now involved."

"Oh no! May dragon fire save us! What can they possibly do against a messenger?"

"They are only doing their jobs, and Chief Lopez is a good man."

"A *good* man? Or a man of worship?"

"A bit of both, actually, but ultimately, a good man."

"Well, that would appear to be that, then. We are now in the hands of… er… what exactly *are* we in the hands of, Fezlet?"

"Time? Fate? Who knows? But let's not underestimate our reluctant hero *just* yet."

"Reluctant?"

"Nobody with an ounce of sanity *wants* to be a hero, but strangely enough, those of the unwilling variety invariably make the best kind."

"That doesn't make sense, really."

"Any foolish chap *aspiring* to be a hero usually ends up as a sticky, bubbling puddle before he's even had a chance to unholster the lance."

"I see."

"Never forget our motto, Simson: 'To be done by others'."

The deputy looked up at the crest. "Eh? I thought our motto was: 'Ignoreth it, and verily it shall goeth away'."

"Each new problem requires circumstance-related, improvised tactics, my friend. Would you care for a Brandy?"

"Don't mind if I do. Starting to get chills down the ol' spine."

"Let go of him, Grindle! You can't possibly strangle anybody in your condition."

"Well, it really gets my goat!"

"You'll get used to it, ol' boy. It's not an easy transition."

"I know, Fazzle... I know." The sigh could not be heard, more *felt*, on the edge of senses. *"But talking about people as though they aren't bloody there."*

Bluebells and Boulders

Svelt awoke. Then, he panicked.

"Oh no. What time is it?"

He ran through the bar, where a far smaller group of trolls were now either drinking, eating, sleeping, gently smouldering, unconscious, or quite possibly… dead.

"Bye, Svelt." Percy's words went unheard as the fretting troll burst out of the inn and into the street.

He'd been lucky—fifteen minutes to get to the flower shop. Plying Vaessa with flowers had crossed his mind, but it seemed inappropriate for a beautiful elf who just happened to work at a florist.

She stood outside Into-Flora as the unmistakable figure of Svelt hurtled into view. He smiled. Her beautiful blue dress not only matched her eyes, but also showed off her perfect figure.

"Evening, Vaessa," he said nervously.

"Hi, Svelt. I like your shirt."

The white, thigh-length shirt had laces crossing a 'V' shape split at the chest, and he did feel different wearing it. "Your dress— *you* look beautiful."

"Thank you."

Svelt offered his arm, which she gratefully accepted. In truth, they did look a bit odd to passers-by. For one thing, Vaessa was a lot taller and slimmer than him—being the more polite example of numerous opposites. A few people recognised her from the shop and nodded appropriately, completely hiding their true feelings, but Vaessa didn't care.

An odd couple. But maybe... oddly perfect.

It was Svelt's first time at a vine bar, and he looked at the sign above as though it was a warning of impending doom.

The Olive Branch.

He braced himself, deciding to take the lead by opening the door for his elven guest, but a smartly dressed man instantly engaged.

"Hi, can we have a tab—"

"I'm sorry... *sir*? We don't allow—" Vaessa guessed what was coming next and stepped in. "Oh, good evening, madam..." the head man instantly changed his manner, as if it were on a switch, "obviously, Ms Flora couldn't make it this evening." He looked disapprovingly at the troll.

"No, Cecil. This is Svelt."

"Charmed, I'm sure... sir," Cecil managed. Svelt got the distinct impression he would not have been allowed in if it hadn't been for Vaessa. "This way, please."

They were led to a cosy little table in a secluded corner of the vine bar, sectioned off with beautifully carved wooden panels. The dancing candlelight seemed to animate them.

"Are you okay, Vaessa?" asked Svelt.

"I'm a bit nervous," she admitted.

"Me too."

Cecil approached again courteously. "Would sir and madam like a drink?" he asked, with various little accompanying gestures that oozed impeccable professionalism.

"*Vaessa*," Svelt hissed, trying to get her attention, "what *is* vine? I've never tried it!"

Cecil looked away and pretended to signal to a waiter. He really was a master of his trade.

"It's made with olives. They put lots of them into a barrel and squeeze really hard until they turn into liquid," she whispered.

"OLIVES!" Heads in the vine bar turned towards them, and the decibel level dropped noticeably—as did the temperature. Cecil smiled and made little shrugging gestures towards the other patrons as if he were conducting an orchestra, cleverly screening the couple as he did so. "Sorry." Svelt stood, holding his hands up in apology to his new audience, somewhat spoiling Cecil's excellent work. This earned him another glare. He sat again. "But Vaessa, I eat olives when I drink beer… like a snack."

"Of course. Olives are fruit, so you *can* eat them, but they also make a delicious drink."

"Really?" Svelt whispered in amazement.

They started giggling.

"Ahem…"

"Yes, sorry, Cecil. May we have a bottle of the *Primadon Ten*, please," she ordered, remembering her last visit with Fiona.

"Excellent choice, madam," Cecil agreed.

"Yes, some of that, please," Svelt chipped in.

"And two glasses, please," added Vaessa.

Cecil walked away with his nose very much in the air.

"Glasses? What, like seeing glassettes?"

"No," she laughed, "they're what you drink vine from."

"Oh, are they?" Svelt asked nervously. "Vaessa, why did you say yes?"

"I'm sorry?"

"I can't help wondering... why did you agree to come out with me?"

"Because I liked you straight away. You didn't pretend to be anything but yourself."

"I don't understand. I can only be a troll— *dwarf troll*. I couldn't be anything else, even if I tried."

"No, I meant your personality, your honesty."

"Hon—"

"You'd be surprised how many men use dishonest methods to try and impress a woman, Svelt. It's something I've only encountered since moving to Landos. The bluebell settled it, I might add. Why did you pick a bluebell?"

"It just seemed right. It reminded me of you."

Cecil approached, balancing the vine bottle on a wooden tray. He placed a glass before each of them. "Would sir like to—" before swivelling around to Vaessa in one silky-smooth motion, "—madam like to sample?"

"No, that's fine, Cecil. Just leave it on the table, please."

"Of course, madam. Would you like to see the menu?"

"In a little while, thank you."

Cecil gave half a bow and walked away.

"What's wrong with him, Vaessa? They don't do that in the taverns or The Cave."

She laughed, realising it was precisely the type of innocent comment she found so attractive about him. "Think of it as a play. Cecil is similar to an actor playing a part. It's expected of him."

Svelt pictured the comical stage play he'd enjoyed in The Squares. "I see," he nodded, trying to understand, as Vaessa filled their glasses.

"To new friends," she said, raising hers above her head.

"Yes," said Svelt, grabbing the delicate object, which instantly shattered in his hand. "Oh no, sorry, Vaessa."

"Don't worry, Svelt."

Out of sheer embarrassment, he blurted the first thing that came to him. "I don't know why it's music to Mr Singe's ears. It's not a very nice sound."

"Eh?"

"Glass breaking. Although, I think Garamanian music is a bit different to most *if* The Banal Spice is anything to go by."

She gave him a puzzled look before signalling to Cecil, who promptly approached the table. He looked sideways at Svelt while dabbing the liquid with a napkin. "Would sir prefer a mug?"

"*No*, another *glass*, please." Vaessa threw him 'the look'—visual daggers with bows on—which only beautiful females can perfect. "Do you ever feel alone, Svelt?"

"I used to all the time, but not so much now. Of course, Mum and Dad were always there for me, but I never had real friends. I mean, there *is* Mrs B. Oh, and Mr Singe… and more recently Don McCon, Ton, Percy, and Rom. Not forgetting Mr Taroo and Mr Sarchy," he added. Vaessa laughed, looking at him as though he were mad. "How about you?"

Cecil returned with a new glass for Svelt. After the last visual reprimand, he felt it best not to comment this time. Vaessa poured some vine into the new glass.

"I have friends here, too, although my family are many miles away."

"Why did you leave them? Why did you come to the city?"

"I just didn't feel as though I belonged in the forest. I wanted to see more of Anglost, I guess."

"Well, we are both here now!"

"Yes, we are," she smiled. "To new friendship," she said, lifting her glass.

Svelt reached out to grab the glass again but stopped just in time. He approached from a different angle, lifting it very gently. "To new friendship," he repeated. They both downed their drinks. Svelt shook his head and spluttered. "It certainly tastes different as a drink!"

"Cecil," Vaessa called quietly.

"Yes, madam?"

"Could we have the menu, please? And another bottle."

"Of course, madam." Cecil wheeled away.

"You'll like the food here, Svelt. It's divine."

"I must admit, Vaessa, I have simple tastes and wouldn't want to hold you back."

"Nonsense! Simple food can still be wonderful."

Svelt looked at the menu Cecil had placed in front of him. It was a *real* piece of parchment and nothing like the cheap, tea-stained copies doing the rounds in The Edges. Neatly folded at the centre from top to bottom, bearing beautifully handwritten content in fresh green ink. The fanciful dish titles meant nothing to him, though the elaborate descriptions made everything sound fantastic. "You decide."

She smiled at him, called Cecil over, and placed an order. The head man promptly returned from the kitchen, gliding to the table with another bottle.

"Where do you live, Svelt? You don't look much like a city boy to me," she asked, much more at ease now.

"No, I live in the country, on a farm. A little place called Turnbridge."

"Turnbridge? And where is that?"

"It's in the southeast, within the borders of Entish, about a two-hour ride from here."

"How wonderful. So, you live on a farm, and what do you do? What's your job?"

"I load the carts," he replied awkwardly.

"With what?"

"Usually with bales, but anything else we can sell in the city, too."

This fascinated Vaessa. The elves of Merewood crafted many beautiful items, but they would never consider trading any of their treasures beyond the woodland realms.

"Things you make yourself?"

"Not so much *make*, er... eggs, meat, milk— oh, there is one thing my dad *does* make. A strange brew that seems to be getting quite popular."

"Fiona makes a nice brew at work sometimes. The leaves are delivered specially from somewhere in the north."

"I don't think there are any leaves in this brew, Vaessa. My dad calls it 'crumple'."

"I'm not sure I like the sound of that."

"Yep! Ol' Barleyso's Crumple!"

A waiter appeared. He carefully set a plate for each of them, then a larger one in the middle of the table containing a small loaf of bread and a block of cheese. Some ready-carved slices of each were neatly arranged to the front. It was garnished with a twiggy branch bearing green fruits, similar in appearance to olives. The waiter also placed two bowls beside them containing a pale green liquid. Svelt obviously recognised the bread and cheese but nothing else.

"Vaessa, what are these?"

"Grapes,"* she answered, "and grape juice."

Grapes were considered a luxury item, whereas olives were not, even though olives came from further afield. Grapes were never to be found on a street market stall. You could be forgiven for thinking they were expensive to produce or transport, hence the exorbitant cost, but this was not the case, as they were nurtured just a short boat trip away across the Angless Canal. The real reason was not one of labour or logistics, more like the Garlicians didn't like the bloody Angless! Feelings were swiftly heading the way of mutuality.

"What do I do with it?" he asked, at a complete loss.

"You take a slice of bread, dip it in the grape juice, then put a slice of cheese on top," she explained, demonstrating at the same time.

"Okay, but what about these little round things?"

"You just eat them whole, like a snack. Like your olives." They tried the food together. "So... why is it called crumple?" she asked.

"I don't know exactly, something to do with the temporary after-effects. It's quite easy to make, though—my dad fills some old barrels with apples and leaves them in the dark for a while."

"What happens after that?"

"Well, he used to add torch fuel to it."

"Torch fuel? Isn't that dangerous?"

"No, he's done it lots of times."

"I *meant* for people to drink!"

"It's quite mild compared to troll brew."

"And what if you haven't got the internal resilience of a troll?"

"Oh, I see what you mean. It's true, some people suffered unfortunate reactions, but others asked him to make it even stronger."

"So, what did he do?"

"The law intervened. They said he couldn't add any other ingredient, and it had to be pure apple fruit."

"Oooh, that must have been a bit scary."

"Yes, it was at first. But a couple of months ago, two nice law officers said he could add anything—to satisfy the growing demand in the city—as long as he paid the correct amount of 'alkee tax'."

The remainder of their date flowed as seamlessly as any involving a troll would allow, and neither wanted it to end.

"Thank you for a wonderful evening, Svelt."

"The pleasure was all mine."

They waited in the warm evening air until her Hacknee cab arrived. Svelt attempted to kiss her hand, but she put her arms around his neck and kissed his cheek instead. He watched the carriage trundle along the well-lit cobbled street until it was beyond sight, not knowing it would soon turn towards shadier suburbs.

Feeling as light as air, he headed to The Cave, joyously acknowledging random people along the way. He was greeted with a warm welcome from everyone on arrival at the inn, *everyone*, that is, remaining upright.

"Svelt! Come an' 'ave a drink with us," insisted Rom.

Bam was right beside him despite their earlier disagreement.

"You know what, I think I will."

"I see you stuck wiv dat shirt den."

"Course. I bought it *for* the date."

"Nah, I meant, you ob-vee-us-lee couldn't get rid of it anywhere."

"Very funny, Rom."

Bam thought so.

"So, who dis boulder on de side den?" asked Rom.

"Nobody you would know."

"I know most of de she-trolls in dis part of town. Where she work?"

Svelt looked from Rom to Bam as Percy carried the beers over. "She's not a troll," he said quietly.

Rom stared at him in disbelief. "Wot? Oh, I get it. She must be dwarf."

"No, she's not a dwarf either," Svelt replied nervously.

The bar quietened, and all eyes seemed to turn towards him. Rom asked the inevitable question: "Wot is she den?"

Svelt looked sheepishly at his drink and downed it in one. "A friend."

*****

The following morning, Svelt sat on his bed and ran through the previous night's events in his head. He wasn't too sure if he was still 'popular Svelt' anymore, as he noticed a slight change in mood from some of his fellow trolls after breaking the news about his date. His mind snapped back into focus.

The map!

He walked through a much quieter bar, with just a few trolls having some liquid breakfast. Nobody acknowledged or even seemed to notice him. Stepping into daylight and the busy street, he found somewhere to sit. Making sure nobody was looking, he took out the piece he had discovered in the library and held it up to the light. Although the page was otherwise blank, a neatly drawn round bottle sat in the left-hand corner—a strange warning sat beneath.

Only the penitent may read from The Lord's book.

The small clock face had reappeared and was pointing again to one. This time, Svelt was at a complete loss. He struggled to make sense of the wording, and the bottle was just a lone symbol, meaning there was no way of knowing where to search. He was beginning to think it was too much for a simple guy like him—way above his head, you might say. His thoughts returned to Vaessa again, and he started to lose concentration.

Svelt sat in the same spot for a long time.

I need to focus—empty my mind of all other thoughts—and the solution will present itself.

Studying the library marker again brought nothing to mind immediately *until* he realised something. The two pieces of paper were identical in shape and size! He pulled out the original map and held it up to the light, revealing numerous buildings represented by squares, then looked at the second piece of paper—the library marker—depicting the bottle on the left-hand side. Holding them both up to the light, he compared. Something was niggling at him, but he couldn't quite put his finger on it.

More time passed, and Svelt was tired of trying to solve the puzzle. He put the two pieces of paper together and opened his belt pouch with an angry tug—it hit him like a hammer!

"How could I have been so stupid?"

Placing the library marker *on top* of the original map aligned them perfectly. He held them aloft once more… and there it was! The bottle and the worded clue appeared *inside* one of the squares to the left half of the map. He now knew which building he sought.

A bottle building?

If the map was an accurate representation of Old Town, then all he had to do was simply follow the route from the library.

Svelt decided to revisit the library. It seemed sensible to ask somebody with knowledge of the area because even *with* the map, he could be going around in circles forever if the building did not display a bottle of some kind. The librarian was undoubtedly an expert on many subjects beyond the mere location of books. With his mind made up, he set off for the library again.

Crossword Clues

"What do you mean you can't find him?" bellowed Chief Lopez. "This man is a murderer!"

"Sorry, sir. When he gave us his statement, he told us he worked in various churches across the city and not much else," explained Frank.

"And we didn't think to ask which ones?"

"He wasn't considered a suspect at the time, and, in all honesty, sir, it wouldn't have mattered. We have been to almost every known church, and nobody has even heard of this man."

"Frank, we…" Lopez said, lowering his voice, "*I* let this man go."

"I understand, sir—he fooled us all. We were blinded by what we assumed was his important position in the church."

"The pry-minister has voiced concerns over this one and wants results."

"Really, sir? I wouldn't have thought—"

"No, no, you're right, Frank. Brutus Stratus has made *his* feelings known, and *he* wants results."

"Oh, dear."

"Right! Go and see Eddi 'The Easel'. Let's get this man's face down on parchment. Then, I want him to copy it ten times, give a copy to every other artist in Old Town and get them to do the same."

"*Real* parchment, sir? That'll cost a slimy sen."*

The coinage of Landos could never be classed as 'pretty'; it had passed through too many devious hands.

"I don't care if he paints it on the back of *The Fast Supper* or some of that greasy stuff Dogban wraps his kababs in. If it can be painted on, use it!"

"Yes, sir."

"Just keep making them, and as soon as we have enough to fill a couple of sacks, start putting them up everywhere."

"How much is the reward, sir?"

"Reward? You know what happens when we offer rewards to the good citizens of Landos, Frank. They start turning their grannies in—even if it requires shaving heads, fitting false beards, and painting hands red. No. There *is* no reward. This is a warning, a plea to the public to keep their eyes open, not a free-for-all witch hunt!"

"Understood, sir."

"This man is far too dangerous. He may have enemies who would be glad to help us, or it may spook him and flush him out. Either way, see to it."

"On it, sir," Frank replied urgently. He left the office to carry out his orders.

"Bert!"

"Yes, sir?" replied the desk officer.

"Send those two idiots in."

"Which ones, sir?"

Fair point. "Dabble and Trubble."

"Yes, sir."

"I've got a nice little job for them," he added quietly to himself, grinning horribly.

*****

Svelt entered the library, estimating he probably had enough time to reach his destination afterwards, assuming the map was reasonably accurate.

"Hello again, sir," said the librarian in a resigned manner, suggesting he wasn't in the least bit surprised to see him again. "How can we help you this time?"

Svelt reluctantly showed the librarian the map. A decision he'd agonised over on the way.

"How fascinating," the librarian said, holding the map up to the light streaming through one of the large windows.

"Do you know this place? The exact location?" Svelt asked, trying to hurry the man.

"Oh yes, sir, no mistaking it. But have you noticed these two symbols on the side here?"

"Yes. Are they important?"

"Could be... depending on your point of view. Where did you get this?"

His question caught Svelt slightly off guard. "A friend drew it for me. It's supposed to make it easier to visit some of the more interesting places in Old Town, but I don't really understand it, to be honest," he admitted.

"A little intricate for that purpose, don't you think? We have excellent maps of the city *here*. Your 'friend' must be a genius, as he appears to have discovered how to draw *inside* paper! Is he a wizard by any chance?"

Svelt tried to look surprised and shook his head. "No."

"Also, I would not call *The Flamin' Bun Bakery* an interesting building," the librarian added with a sneer.

"What? *Flamin' Bun?*"

"Yes, I believe it is a play on words. Some of our chirpy neighbours in The Edges—the east end of Landos—are making up their own little language."

"I don't understand...?"

"Flamin' Bun, sir... sun! It is another way of referring to the city's favourite cake—our very own humble *sun*—in the form of rhyme. Most amusing."

"I see. Why not just say the word 'sun'? It's a lot easier *and* quicker."

"Who knows how the minds of our east-side cousins work. It seems to keep them amused... at least, between the muggings."

"Do they have a rhyme for *all* words?"

"They appear to be working towards it."

"Well, what about the loon, then?" Svelt asked, temporarily forgetting the urgency of his visit.

"It doesn't rhyme with a cake, sir."

"Oh, I didn't think of that."

"But that is only a problem if you own a bakery. As you've asked, I believe they *do* have a rhyming word for the loon. I think—and I may be wrong—it is known in cocky rhyming terms as the 'full moon'."

"What's a *moon*?"

"Best not to ask. Without going into detail, I believe it refers to a part of the anatomy hilariously exposed during drunken tavern games."

"Anat—"

"*Rounded* part of the anatomy."

"Ah, got you. What's so funny about exposing your b—"

"As I said, sir, no need for details—"

"—elly?"

The librarian shook his head. "Anyway, back to the point. This drawing shows many buildings, sir, but not all are important. Like, The Flamin' Bun Bakery, for example."

"Okay, so can you help me then?" Svelt asked a little desperately.

"You can trust the map. It is accurate for location purposes—if a little crude. The building you require is *Sant Jon's Church*, three streets from here." The librarian ran his finger across the page to illustrate the direction from the library.

"I plotted the direction easily enough, but... Church? What's a bottle—"

"Bottle? There are other, much *older* names for it. The water carrier symbolises G— our lord, sir."

"Thank you." Svelt attempted to take the papers, but the librarian gripped them slightly harder to look at the symbols again. "Please, I need to get going."

"Have you considered the clue?"

"No, but I shall work it out. Thank you again for your help."

"Not at all." The librarian released his grip. Svelt put the map pieces away. "If I were you, sir, I would exercise extreme caution." The man's usual matter-of-fact tone took on a slightly sinister edge.

"I shall."

He dropped a coin into the box, and the librarian watched him leave. Almost immediately after the troll's departure, the serial book stamper left his desk, walked straight past the ends of many bookcases, and disappeared down one of the aisles near the end of the building.

Svelt hurried along the streets. He had the overall direction in his mind and hoped he'd got it right.

*****

Shajar-wah emerged from the corridor like a shadow. He was holding a book. Upon entering the main room of the church building, he moved cautiously towards a pedestal, scanning the room and listening intently all the while. Easing to the back of the small wooden stand, he carefully set the book upon it. He stepped back slightly, emitting a small sigh of relief.

One final touch.

Inching to the side, hunched on all fours, he leaned over and gently placed a red velvet cushion at the splayed feet before retreating slowly to safer ground. He didn't entirely straighten when he stood but almost loped to the back of the hall, where he hid behind a column.

The Master of Sant Jon's left his office and headed out of the main door into the town. The church doors were never closed during the day because there was no need. The simple building held nothing of value other than the books in the library. If you were so bold as to steal from a house of worship, you would undoubtedly receive everything you deserve.

Svelt arrived at his destination. Despite the sign, which, until recently, he had not associated with a holy place, it did not bear the hallmarks of a church. There were no windows of coloured glass, impressive arched doorways or artistic masonry. Just a rectangular building that reminded him a little of Don McCon's—without the monstrous window. It was obviously nowhere near as old as the surrounding buildings, and he wondered what had stood there in ages gone by. The only 'characteristic' feature was the divine water carrier (a simple bottle made from the dried skin of a large fruit) crudely painted onto a plain sign of rough wood.

Just as he was about to enter, he noticed the two symbols from his map; they were tiny and had been delicately etched into the stone, fitting neatly onto a small brick—an eye above a triangle. Both were encompassed by a band of silver. At least he now knew he was in the right place.

Standing in the small hall of Sant Jon's Church, Svelt took in his surroundings—a pedestal atop a speaking platform being the main focal point. As with the exterior, everything was severely bland and noticeably lacking in decorative artwork of any kind. Several long benches were facing the elevated platform. To the right stood another unremarkable pedestal with a red velvet cushion at its feet. It also displayed a book. Svelt was puzzled. This wasn't really what he'd been expecting. The clue mentioned a book, and, looking around, he could see no other, so he assumed it to be the one. He edged towards it, and the wooden floor creaked horribly under his weight.

Shajar-wah looked on in fascination and stirred excitedly in the comfort of his hiding place.

No set outcome to this part of the game. This is a test!

Svelt remembered the librarian's words: "Have you considered the clue?" *Only the penitent may read from The Lord's book.* He had no idea of the meaning, but a book stood before him, and he assumed another clue would be tucked inside the pages. Trying hard to focus, he couldn't understand the significance of the cushion set before the pedestal. A heavy tension hung in the air, even though it was broad daylight. The creaking floorboards only added to his apprehension, so he trod, as carefully as a troll can, around the edge instead—sidling along the wall. Shajar-wah almost shrieked with surprise and had to stop himself from clapping his hands in delight. Svelt got that feeling again—someone or *something* was watching him. He edged along the wall, approached the rear of the pedestal, and gently lifted the book. Drawing a deep breath, he closed his eyes as if *expecting* something nasty to happen. Nothing. Turning the book over in his hands, he looked at the cover. To his surprise, the title was not *The Lord's Book* but boldly stated *The Truth*. Svelt had no interest in small details this time, and holding the book 'spine upwards' in one hand, he thumbed through the many pages with the other. After a couple of seconds, a piece of paper fluttered gently to the floor. Shajar-wah could barely contain his surprise. Although the unlikeliest of figures standing before him was clearly not a creature of science, nor was he a creature of religion. The troll had most unexpectedly passed the test and earned the right to view the artefact!

Svelt carefully picked up the piece of paper. It held no surprise for him now being identical to the other two. He didn't pause to examine it further, putting it straight into his pouch instead. He returned the book gently to the pedestal and edged out of the building, hugging the wall.

The master returned, entered the church without a sideways glance, and headed towards his office.

Shajar-wah was still hiding; he was in dangerous territory now. The uncompromising laws of *time* demanded that he recover the book, but instead, he waited… something told him to wait.

*****

"Barny, you idiot!"

"Sorry, Fred."

Barny tried unsuccessfully to scrape glue back into the pot he had just knocked over.

"I am not going all the way back to the station to get more glue... no way!" said Fred.

"Well, *I* ain't," said Barny grumpily.

"*You* knocked it over."

"Why don't we jus' dump some o' these drawings and go for a beer?"

Fred looked down at the rough sketches of the evil-looking, bald-headed holy man. "No, Barny, this is important. Anyway, there ain't that many to put up till they make some more, *and* we are already in enough bloody trouble, fanks to you... Trubble!"

" 'ow's anyone s'posed to recognise 'im from these scribbles? I thought Eddi was meant to be good."

"To be 'onest, 'e's better when 'e's got somefing to copy from, like... art, an' money, an' that."

"Look, we 'aven't got enough glue now, but I know a neat little trick to make some more... sort of," said Barny, spotting a Bakery.

"Wot's a *sort* o' glue?" Fred asked, eyeing him suspiciously.

"It's like normal glue, but not *quite* as strong."

"Are you sure?"

"Absolutely. And it will save you 'aving to go all the way back to the station and explain to the chief."

"Me? But you knocked it over."

"Yeah, but you are the top-rankin' officer 'ere."

"We are both standard law officers... same rank!"

"Yeah, but the chief respec's you more, 'e told me."

Fred tried to turn his collar up and square his shoulders—it was a valiant attempt... on both counts. "Well, yeah, stands to reason, I s'pose. Okay, Barny, whadda we do?" asked Fred, already giving in.

"Wellll, if we make our way to *The Pig and Napkin*, I'll show you."

"The Pig and Napkin?"

"Yeah."

"Why The Pig and Napkin?"

The law officers strolled side by side, already heading in the general direction despite Fred's question.

" 'cos they've got all the basic ingredients you need to make glue," explained Barny.

"Like wot?"

"Beer, Fred... beer."

"Beer? 'ow can you *sort of* make glue out o' beer?"

"Don't fink you can," admitted Barny as they walked past the bakery. "But it'll 'elp me figger out where I can nick some flour from."

*****

The tall, snake-like man moved stealthily, keeping to the shadows until he arrived at the Church of Sant Jon.

"The creature was here. I know it."

He did not feel comfortable. Preparing to enter the building, he noticed the two symbols engraved into the brick. It was like a flaming brand to his eyes, and he crossed the threshold quickly.

"This cannot be right."

Puzzling over the strange layout of the building, he was unable to grasp a concept or belief even vaguely reminiscent of his lord's teachings. Nor his own precious, ancient memories. Shajar-wah watched him with interest. Eventually, the holy man's eyes fell upon an object of familiarity, crude still, in written form, but comforting nonetheless. Pedestal with velvet cushion in place, as it should be. He was slightly annoyed to see the book unopened with no page on display, merely closed and unloved as if it had been put there without any care.

I shall soon fix that.

"Hey, friend... my son. Can I help you?" came a nearby voice.

Zeqar rolled his eyes. Although time was never his enemy, interference was beginning to thin his patience, but... this *was* a holy man. "I merely wish to pray, Father."

The master looked puzzled. "*Father*? We do not have—" he cut short, noticing the pedestal, and wondered how the cushion had got there.

Zeqar turned sharply and drew his dagger, all in one smooth movement. "Father, we are both men of The Lord. I mean you no harm, but I have a higher purpose." He ushered the master back to his office, using the dagger as an incentive. "Sit."

"I don't understand."

"You don't need to. Just obey, and you will not be harmed." Zeqar looked around and spotted some rope hanging from a curtain. He cut a length with his dagger, bound the master's arms behind his back and tied the remainder to the chair. "Please, do not try to move."

Zeqar returned to the hall and headed straight for the pedestal. The floor creaked beneath his feet, but he wasn't paying attention, staring at the book instead. As he neared, the title became clearer. "*The Truth*? How dare they?" Now striding angrily, the ominous creaking became a resounding *crack*, and the floorboards gave way beneath him. Before any cries or words of surprise left his mouth, Zeqar fell a long way... to his death.

Shajar-wah emerged from his hiding place. He moved quickly to the pedestal and retrieved the book before loping awkwardly along the corridor past the master's office. He entered the small library, and the air began to crackle.

*****

Heading back to The Hard Rock Cave, something jogged Svelt's memory. He stopped and sat at a table outside a small tea shop. When he realised table service wasn't forthcoming, he went inside and ordered a hot drink. "Would you happen to have a quill and parchment, please?" he asked.

"Yes, I'll bring them over to you," the owner said, looking slightly put upon. Svelt waited patiently. After a while, the owner appeared with his drink. He turned to the counter and presented Svelt with a quill, inkpot, and a few order-taking parchlets. "Sorry, best I can do," he explained.

"That's fine, thank you." A few moments of thoughtful planning were required before Svelt began to fill the small papers with his craggy handwriting. He sipped his drink while scribbling away, even daring to ask for some more parchlets, to which the owner somewhat reluctantly agreed. Now, he just needed to find a parchman,* which wouldn't be too difficult in his present location.

A parchman would swiftly deliver your written words anywhere in the city for an agreed fee.

Checking back over his strained written efforts, he made several minor adjustments, hoping to avoid embarrassing himself or letting his fellow dwarves and trolls down. After all, the intended recipients were of much higher standing.

The parchman jogged away with papers in hand as Svelt finished his drink and left the tea shop. It had been another eventful day.

Before entering The Cave, Svelt pulled out the marker discovered in the church. As it was again identical in shape and size, there was only one course of action. Laying it over the original map, ensuring the edges were correctly aligned, he held it up to the light. What he saw made him laugh out loud—the librarian had been wrong! The Flamin' Bun Bakery *was* an important building, after all. It was also quite close to Sant Jon's Church.

Svelt noticed something different about this particular marker. Firstly, the clock face was not present. Secondly, the two symbols—previously displayed on the left-hand border—were now *inside* the square representing the bakery.

If there is no indication of time, then when should I visit?

The only other addition was a simple line drawing, which he assumed were steps.

This is not going to be easy. What do I look for when I enter the bakery? Should I just be direct and ask if they know what the symbols mean?

Another thought struck him as he looked at the number of squares on the map. He'd always felt he was being watched while trying to solve the puzzles.

What if I was not meant to go any further? Whoever was setting the clues could easily send me to an empty building, a dead-end… or worse!

He shuddered at the thought.

"No doubt I shall find out tomorrow," he said quietly.

Dates with Death

There are usually two reasons for a troll to 'stride purposefully'. Either platters of food have been made available on a 'help yourself/first come' basis, *or* someone is about to get hit… very hard. Sometimes, the two are related. A third *has* reared its ugly head on rare occasions, but, as a rule, they don't like to talk about it, and the purposeful strider would prefer to explain it away as one of the former.

The Squares came into view. The place was a hive of activity and as hectic as ever.

"Hey, Svelt!"

Doc Taroo waved frantically from the front of his stall.

"Hi, Mr T!" Svelt called back.

"Please, call me Doc!"

"Sorry, Doc!"

"Got some great new shirts, lad! *Almost* in your size, too!" Doc cried hopefully.

Svelt continued walking.

"Maybe tomorrow, Mr T! Sorry, Doc… Doc!" He waved and melted into the crowd.

Liv Taroo made her way to the front of the stall with an expectant look, but Doc shook his head despondently, and she disappeared again.

Svelt eventually emerged from the sea of bodies and entered The Inside Market, hoping the jewellery stall was still there. He was relieved to find it in the same place.

"Hello again," the lady smiled. "I must be doing something right."

"My mum loved the charms—she thought they were beautiful. Thank you."

"You're welcome. How can I help today?"

"I am looking for something for my friend, er... she is a girl."

"Young love, eh?"

"Er... wellll..."

"Try over here," she laughed, "I've got some beautiful items for the *younger* woman."

Svelt slowly scanned the jewellery display, but nothing really stood out—nothing special enough. He withdrew his gaze in slight disappointment when something caught his eye. It lit his face in much the same way as that first sight of Vaessa had.

"I would like to buy that, please."

*****

"Well, I don't know why you're bothering, darling. He is clearly not good enough for you."

"We've already been through all this, Fiona. What exactly does 'good enough' mean anyway?"

Fiona tried a different approach.

"*Vaessa*... you are beautiful, charming, elegant.... *perfect*. And *him*... well!"

"I've told you before, Fiona, it's my decision. I know you mean well and have always been there, for which I'll always be grateful, but the kind of guy *you* have in mind is just not right for me. I choose Svelt!"

Svelt approached the shop cautiously after hearing his name mentioned among slightly raised voices.

"Very well, dear," sighed Fiona.

The little bell rang as the door opened.

"Svelt!"

She rushed over and threw her arms around his neck, prompting an utterly disapproving look from Ms Flora.

"Hello, ladies."

He smiled at Fiona.

"Hello," she replied unenthusiastically before retreating to the back office.

"Is everything okay, Vaessa?"

"Yes, of course. What have you been up to?" she asked, quickly changing the subject.

"Oh, I have... been looking at some of the interesting buildings in Old Town," he managed.

"Really, which ones?"

"Er... the bakery!"

"The *bakery*?" Vaessa laughed. "Well, that figures," she said, patting his stomach.

"Haha, yes. So... Vaessa, would you like to go out again tomorrow night? I understand if it's too soon."

"I'd love to."

"That makes me so happy. Where shall we go?"

A long, exaggerated clearing of the throat came from somewhere in the background.

"It's your turn, Svelt. You choose," she insisted.

"But I only know taverns and inns. None of them are good enough for you."

"Oh, so there are some brains in there somewhere. *Hmmph.*"

"Sorry, Fiona?"

"Nothing, dear."

Vaessa smiled. "Svelt, I want to go where *you* go. Meet the people *you* know."

"The Cave? I don't know, Vaessa. It's not real—"

"Come on! It'll be fun."

"Okay, if you're sure. What time do you want me to pick you up?"

"I'll meet you there. Where is it?"

"That's not a good idea. Please, at least let me meet you here. We can walk—it's not far."

"Okay, meet me here at seven."

"I certainly will. Oh, I almost forgot, this… is for you."

He handed her a pretty little box bound with blue ribbons. She carefully loosened the ties, opened it, and gasped.

"It's beautiful."

Almost in tears, she held a silver chain so light in colour that it was closer to white. Hanging from it was a small sapphire.

"The bluebell reminded me of you, and the sapphire reminds me of your eyes."

"Oh, *Svelt*."

She pecked him on the cheek, and he was gone.

Fiona emerged from the back of the shop.

"It *is* beautiful," she admitted. She took Vaessa's hand in hers. "If you're happy, darling, I'm happy too."

*****

Death hurtled through the blackness. The speed and distance were beyond calculation, but, in *reality*, it was instantaneous. He emerged from the silky-smooth momentum of the void directly into the present. The impact of his form hitting time-reliant normality was astronomical, causing friction even asteroids would be proud of. Very few had ever witnessed it. Because to do so was to cheat Death himself.

The motionless form of his unsuspecting, soon-to-be-enlightened pupil was lying on the ground, having just fallen from a great height. Death was upon him before the stricken man could even lift his head. He brought his trusty scythe around in a sweeping arc— there was an almighty clash of steel. Before even attempting to stand, the man had nullified Death's right and very purpose!

The hooded apparition reeled in amazement and disbelief.

Now, the scythe came down straight from above—there was no time for artistry *here*. The blow was easily deflected again with nothing more than a *dagger*.

The power behind the parried strike planted a rare seed of doubt.

Perhaps this 'man' cannot be released from his earthly ties.

The reaper of souls had been given one job and one job only. The fact that it was very repetitive *and* would last for all eternity was irrelevant. He was always there at the end—the choice was not his. Raising the scythe ten times quicker than a man could blink, he felt the steel of the dagger against his bones before he had even begun to bring the blade down. Death bowed his head.

"I don't know how you resist, but Death is... er, I mean, *I*... am inevitable! If not today, then tomorrow. If not *tomorrow*, then a thousand years from now!" He bellowed the words with absolute confidence.

Zeqar smiled. "You said that to me *two* thousand years ago, my friend."

"What?"

Death placed his scythe against a wall. He was not used to asking questions—he was more at home with people crying '*Why?*' to their reacquainted friends after his *mostly* unappreciated handiwork.

"We both do The Lord's bidding. I cannot kill you any more than you can kill me."

Death thought about this.

The unexpected delay caused by the man's arrogant, blatant, and downright *rude* refusal to die caused his black-robed form to shimmer as he tended to 'business' simultaneously in millions of different locations. Not to mention dimensions.

Zeqar waited patiently.

Death returned from his thoughts—and a simple, cushy little number where the recipient of *reasonably* bad news accepted his fate without so much as a gripe or minor protestation. No daggers, either.

"*So*… immortal then?" asked Death.

"Hmmm, more… *recyclable*, really."

"I see. Well, do you fancy going a few rounds anyway?" grinned Death (intentionally on this occasion), hopping around erratically in a rough circle and shadowboxing with excited anticipation. For *him*, it was usually such a one-sided affair.

"Alas, I am pressed for time…"

Death raised a metaphoric eyebrow…

"… in the mortal world, I mean, you understand." Zeqar shrugged. "Besides, we would be at it all century."

"True," moaned Death.

A blinding white light illuminated the vast chamber momentarily, leaving the glum reaper alone in the dark—billions of lost, wandering souls aside, naturally. Purely out of habit, he lifted the quill to cross out the name and watched with a little shudder as it disappeared from the scroll. "Gives me the creeps when that happens. Hmmm, Zeqar... I *do* remember him now. It was at The Temple of Horny Boar, in Wasgard." He revisited the scene in his mind... there was Zeqar, explaining to the chieftain warlord—in the strongest possible terms—that raping, pillaging, and brutal violence amounted to unacceptable behaviour. Much to everyone's surprise, he said this *after* removing Boar's axe from his skull, simultaneously wielding his dagger. Luckily, Death's appearance, although slightly misjudged, had not been totally in vain.

"*Zeqar*. Always was a cheating little sod!"

"Aye, that he was," agreed Horny Boar of Wasgard, appearing at Death's side holding his neck. "I was just starting to enjoy meself too."

*****

Svelt bowled into The Cave.

"Drinks all round!" he cried.

A huge cheer followed.

"Svelt back!" shouted Rom.

"Sit down, pal," Percy signalled to Svelt. "I'll bring dem over."

After serving what seemed like a never-ending and sometimes *repeating* line of trolls, Percy placed a tray of beers on Svelt's table. Most trolls ordered at least two beers at a time, and in Svelt's case, it saved Percy's legs, too.

"Percy, can I speak to you for a minute?"

"Sure, wot wrong, friend?"

Percy sat next to him.

"Tomorrow, I am bringing a girl here."

" 'ERE!" shouted Percy. "Sorry, sorry. Here?"

"Yes, she really wanted to meet you all."

"Svelt. Now, don't tink I rude but, well, you not big like troll and you got no beard like dwarf..."

"It's okay, Percy... carry on."

"...well, I was finking... wot's your girl like? We don't get many she-trolls in 'ere anyway, but if she a dwarf—"

"Don't worry, Percy. She's not a dwarf, but she is *different*."

"How?"

"She is tall, with beautiful pale skin, silver hair, and blue eyes."

"Percy! We dyin' of furst over 'ere!" shouted Bam.

"Good! I stay over 'ere den!" Percy shouted back.

He gave a puzzled look, but before he could say anything, Svelt beat him to it.

"She's an elf," he revealed quietly.

Percy thought carefully for a moment, which can sometimes be painful for a troll. "Well, that *will* be a first, but rest assured, she will be made to feel most welcome in *this* humble establishment, my friend."

Svelt stared at Percy.

"Your speech. You spoke *differently*."

"When you own a place like this, it pays to do as the customers do."

Svelt stared again.

"Owner?"

"Yes, Svelt, *owner*. Being a barman gives you a fascinating insight into what customers really think. Now, as your host, I shall make sure your young lady will be made to feel very welcome. I've just got to try and explain it to these morons."

Percy smiled at Svelt and placed an olive on a stick in each beer. Svelt beamed back.

"Thanks, Percy."

"Only for you, pal."

Percy attempted to wink—unfortunately, it looked like he was having some kind of seismic seizure.

"Percy at it again, lads!" cried Bam.

This was greeted with a cheer.

"If you don't shut it…" said Percy, "I'm gonna ram dat mug where de bun don't shine!"

Another cheer.

Svelt smiled. He felt more at home than he had ever done. The olive population was about to get dangerously close to extinction.

Bread and Water

You had to admire the chairwoman's persistence. Attempting to instil urgency and enthusiasm by calling an 'emergency' meeting at an ungodly hour could have been a stroke of genius. It wasn't. The usual response of dubious excuses found their way to her desk. An exhausted Natonya was awoken by the committee members filtering in mid-morning at their leisure.

"Good, er... yes... *morning*. Sorry to summon you all at such *short* notice, but we've had an anonymous proposal."

"Who said that?"

The question prompted a loud cheer.

"Haha, nice one, Henry!"

"Nice one, what?" asked Henry, already confused.

"By *anonymous*, I mean the proposal arrived via a parchman. We don't know where it came from," the chairwoman explained.

"Parchman? Members of the street rabble aren't allowed to put forward suggestions. That's why *we're* here. That's *why* we scrapped the vote," Cedric pointed out.

"Yes, but this is a good idea and would also bring in extra revenue."

"Fair enough, can't argue with extra revenue. I'm a little bit ribby this week," another voice declared.

"Not for us *personally*. Extra revenue for the good of the city," the chairwoman pointed out.

"You can't go letting the general public have ideas. In my experience, that's not beneficial to our existence," warned Cedric.

"S'right," agreed Olaf. "You start letting people have ideas, and before you know it, they'll be dragging us into the street, cutting bits off, and setting fire to stuff. Trust me, I've been around a few uprisings in my time."

"Bits? What *kind* of bits, exactly?" asked Henry.

"Important ones."

Henry, whose hearing dramatically improved when it concerned his personal well-being, raised his eyebrows. "I vote we ignore this proposal, Madam Chairwoman... I need my bits! Especially the important ones."

"Aye!"

"Aye!"

"That was a very long time ago," she reassured them. "We have come a long way since then."

Chief Lopez didn't attend many meetings as he felt too much time was wasted before any real progress was made. His feelings were already glancing at the door and waiting *impatiently* for *any*, let alone 'real'. Before anybody else uttered a pointless remark, his commanding voice rose above the squabbling din.

"May we hear what the proposal suggests, Madam Chairwoman?"

"Yes, of course, chief." She was glad of the interruption. "The idea involves employing official guards to patrol the river, thereby preventing people from throwing rubbish, or 'pee-loosing' it by any other means."

"What's *pee-loosing* mean?" asked Henry, his curiosity momentarily overcoming any fear of a potential loss of bits. Even important ones.

"It is an act of defacement upon our river. Or, indeed, anywhere else. It derives from the word *pee-loose-on*, which our anonymous contributor has named the rubbish. In this instance, the pee-loose-on could be debris from the boats, paper thrown in by passers-by, or… bodily fluids," she explained.

"Bodily fluids? But isn't that where all the sh— er, waste from the sewers ends up anyway? Not to mention bodies, eh, Cedric?"

Cedric ignored Olaf's wink and the annoying grin, casually checking his nails instead.

"Yes, but that is *achieved* in a dignified manner, from the privacy of home. Well, for some, anyway. If not home, then the public places dotted around the city," she explained.

This prompted a murmur of general understanding among the members.

"Therefore, we can't have people simply throwing, spilling, or emptying anything *directly* into the river from the banks, you see."

Chief Lopez could see where this was going. It would inevitably involve charging or taxing people in one way or another, so he decided to cut to the chase again.

"Sorry to interrupt again, madam."

"*Yes*, chief?" Her tone suggested she was slightly put out this time.

"Where *exactly* did this idea come from?"

"As I said, Mr Lopez, unfortunately, there was no name. The writer had simply scribbled… er… let me just check… SveltHam fest, at the bottom. We are still trying to pinpoint this location using our records."

"Sveltham fest?" the chief repeated. "May I see the paper?"

"Of course."

The chairwoman handed the parchlets to the chief. He read through them carefully, and his eyes settled on the scribble at the bottom.

"Sveltham fest." Something stirred in his mind. "Svelt… ham… *fest*? Fist! Oh sh—" he slapped his forehead, grabbed his coat, and headed for the door. It slammed shut behind him.

The chairwoman was flabbergasted. "That man is impossible!"

By now, the mumbling and chattering around her had developed into full-blown squabbling again. Giving up on any possibility of restoring order, she stood on a chair to regain their attention for a split second. "I RESIGN!"

The door slammed shut behind her. The room fell deadly silent, and the members looked at one another. Ronald, who had been sitting unnoticed in the corner since the meeting began—possibly several of the previous ones, too—stopped colouring in, looked up at the others and shook his head disapprovingly. "Wimmin's problems."

*****

It had been a *very* good night. Svelt sat at the bar with a strong, dark, treacle-like drink and a rock-splitting headache. Once again, he tried hard to focus on the test before him but didn't feel up to it. It now seemed like an age since the wizard had given the map to him, but that was before a bright, beautiful light appeared at the end of the long, dark tunnel. He fully appreciated the importance of his inherited quest, but all he could see right now was Vaessa. He leaned back.

"I could always throw it away."

"Wassat, Svelt?" called Percy while collecting empties from the tables.

"Nothing, Percy, just talking to myself."

"Wimmin, me friend," he sighed, "dat wot dey do to you."

"Sure is, pal," Svelt agreed, going along with it.

The third marker differed from the others, and the weary troll felt this would be the last hurdle to *whatever* lay in wait. Although the day ahead was guaranteed to include a bakery visit, fluffy bread didn't hold quite the same weight as proper troll fayre.

"Percy? I've a feeling I'm not going to be around much today. Any chance of a snack before I go?"

"You know I don't do food orders, Svelt. Grub ain't up for a couple of hours yet."

"Come on, Percy, I've got some important business to take care of— I probably won't even have time to eat."

"Dere always time to eat," insisted Rom, who was also feeling slightly the worse for wear.

"Go out to de kitchen an' see Mrs Tolly-Brijes. She might 'ave some rock bakes ready."

"Thanks, Percy."

"Dat ain't fair!" moaned Rom. "We gotta wait for ours."

Percy produced two mugs of molt he'd already poured in anticipation. "Is it fair now?"

Rom held a mug in each hand. "It gettin' *fairer*."

Svelt thanked Mrs Tolly-Brijes and left The Cave via the kitchen, munching the rock bakes as he walked along. "Right, let's get this over and done with."

*****

Brutus Stratus hurried towards the pry-minister's residence in the recently named area of Drowning Street—the committee members were on something of a roll now. The name referred to days of yore when it led directly to the river and was used to escort protestors—or self-appointed opposition leaders—away from the ruler's abode. Once at the riverside, they were given a fair, albeit short, chance to rethink the placement of their loyalties. The inability to breathe can bring about a miraculous clarity of mind in the decision-making department.

As he swiftly rounded a corner, the deputy almost trod on a bearded man sitting cross-legged on the ground, back propped against a wall, clutching a small metal pot. He peered up at the giant figure through thick, round glassettes.

"Are you okay, my good man? What are you doing down there?"

"I'm 'omeless, sir. The ground is my bed."

"Homeless? But surely Landos is your home, is it not?"

" 'utless, sir, I meant to say 'utless."

"I see, how unfortunate. Well, must dash, I'm late for—"

"Please, sir, before yeh go… spare a quart for an 'ome— man of limited shelter."

"Oh, I'm not sure if I… aha! You are in luck, my good fellow! Well, in a manner of speaking, of course."

Brutus tossed the small coin into the man's tin—which responded with a hollow, lonely echo—and started on his way again.

"Gord bless, sir… Evan awaits yeh."

Brutus stopped and turned back to face the man.

"*Gord*? Have you not been educated, sir? Oh, of course, my apologies. It is the slang accent of the east side," Brutus remarked, shaking his head. "Silly me. Good day, sir. Unusual hat, by the way."

"Fank yeh, sir. Keeps the rain off, see."

The man watched the bulky troll move with surprising agility along the street until he reached the heavily guarded house. He swept inside unchallenged.

"East side? Wot's 'e goin' on about? I'm from… er… out of town."

The beggar applied some more thought.

"An' 'ow else can yeh say it? Gord's 'is bloody name." He retrieved the coin, which held slightly less trading value than a dog-end after a pigeon had finished with it, and flipped it into the air.

"*Evan… awaits.*"

Victor sat on his bed, randomly moving delicately carved wooden figures around on a board of black and white squares. It was beginning to frustrate him. A loud knock at the door broke his already strained concentration.

"Enter."

Brutus stomped across the tiled room.

"Afternoon, sir."

"You really must get some quieter footwear, Brutus."

"These are my feet, sir. Unfortunately, shoes do not seem to outlast the day, but I shall look into other options. Perhaps thick, luxurious rugs are in order?"

"Splendid idea. Do they make them in your size?"

"No, I… never mind. Apologies for my timekeeping. I have been interacting with the general public."

"Marvellous! How is he?"

"No, I think you mis—"

"No doubt another medal is in order then—heroic deeds aplenty again, I presume?"

"I beg your pardon, I— ah, I see where we may have our pipework crossed. No, pry-minister, I wasn't referring to General 'Soaky' Publick."

"You weren't?"

"No, sir. I meant that on the way here, I conversed freely with a person of the streets."

"Oh, I'm sorry to hear that, Brutus."

"Anyway, I have some interesting news. A proposal, in fact."

"Is that it? Another boring proposal?"

"Well, yes, b—"

"Not now, Brutus, can't you see I'm trying to learn… what's this game called again?"

"Stress, sir," sighed Brutus, rolling his eyes.

"And what is it you have to do? Remind me of the objective."

"You must eliminate as many enemy pieces as possible—while protecting your own—and surround the opposition leader, thereby forcing him into submission. The successful player will use fiendishly clever tactics and forward planning to achieve this goal."

"Yes, of course. Okay, Brutus, my old friend, what's the problem?"

"The committee has put forward a rather excellent proposal regarding the state of the river," Brutus explained.

"State? It's got to be all *watery*, or the boats won't work properly."

"No, sir, not liter— well, actually, that is *exactly* the point!"

"Is it?" beamed Victor, feeling very pleased with himself.

"The river is becoming *less watery* due to the growing amount of rubbish being thrown into it," simplified Brutus.

"So, what do we do?"

"The committee has agreed on a proposal which involves employing a small team of guards. In the first instance, their job would be to clean up the river using nets while standing on floating platforms. When there is less pee-loose-on, their job will be to stop people filling it up again."

Victor didn't understand all the words but thought he had spotted some mistakes. "Why don't we just get the law to do it?"

"Because, although pee-loose-on is unacceptable, it is not a major crime, and therefore, not worthy of their valuable time. They are terribly busy, sir."

At that moment, an image returned to the deputy's mind. A vague recollection of two law officers— slightly the worse for wear—arguing about glue. He happened across them one evening after slipping out for a rare beverage.

"Most of them," he added.

"Well, why don't we make it stricter than 'unacceptable' and just lop a few heads off?"

"Pry-minister, we have come such a long way. I'm sure a stern ticking off will suffice and start to sink in slowly… if you'll forgive the pun. After all, people have been slowly destroying the river in this manner for decades."

"What about the cost? Who's paying for all this?" Victor asked triumphantly.

"Anybody caught in the act of pee-loosing the river will be fined by the guards. We shall also tax traders for using the docks."

"Isn't that a bit unfair?"

"Not at all, sir. Most of the debris is caused *by* the traders."

"Well, I must say, the committee is doing rather well lately."

"Actually, this proposal was suggested by the public."

"I knew it, he—"

"Not the General, sir, a normal, everyday fellow."

"Oh, really? Where is he then? We must reward him," Victor suggested, feeling really important now.

"Nobody knows, but he has a name… of sorts."

"Don't we have records? To check who this fellow is?"

"Yes, sir. That is the next course of action. Very time-consuming, though, so as long as you are happy, we can proceed."

"Brutus?"

"Yes, sir?"

"Do *you* think it's a good idea?"

Oh, and he was doing so well. "Yes, sir, it's an excellent idea."

"Very well then."

Victor signed his name on the large parchment.

"Thank you. Now, if you will excuse me, your most reviled ignorance, I have work to do."

Victor beamed with pride. "Of course. Thank you, Brutus."

"Not at all, sir."

Victor watched the huge deputy leave the room and resumed stress tactics. He picked up the heaviest black figure and knocked every white piece from the board, punching the air triumphantly as he looked down at them scattered across the floor.

"If something is in your way, simply remove it," he said with a shrug. He thought about this for a moment and then corrected himself. "Simply *have it removed.*"

*****

Svelt headed in the direction of the bakery. Although it was a warm day, the heavy clouds gathering overhead made it feel like rain was trying its best to escape but couldn't quite make it. It was as busy as ever on the streets, with people rushing everywhere and carts trundling along the cobbles. He looked around vacantly.

Is this what I really want? Or life on the farm? Let's solve this artefact puzzle, and then time to meet Vaessa. What is *an artefact anyway?*

As he neared the bakery, Svelt became increasingly agitated with each step.

What am I supposed to do when I get there? It is just a bakery, after all.

The third marker showed steps, but symbols aside, he had nothing else to go on. Bracing himself, he opened the door of The Flamin' Bun Bakery. A large, friendly-looking lady wearing a white apron stood behind the counter.

"Hello, sir. How can I help you?"

He was a little surprised by her accent, as he had been expecting a raw, cocky greeting after the librarian's lessons concerning the regional dialects of Landos.

"I... er... your accent. I assumed you'd be from the east end."

"The sign?"

"Yes."

"Just a bit of fun, sir. I have brothers in The Edges, and one of them suggested it."

"I see."

"So...?"

Svelt desperately scanned the tiny interior, with only seconds to try and spot something important.

"Just a loaf of bread, please," he replied uselessly.

"Can I tempt you to some cakes too? They *are* the city's favourite... freshly baked."

"Er... no, not re—"

"But these are our very own speciality... carrot suns!"

"Okay, sure. Why not."

"You won't regret it, sir. I promise."

"I've regretted it ever since I took it from him."

"I'm sorry?"

"Nothing, just talking to myself."

"Okay, I'll just get your items."

"Excuse me, madam."

"Yes?"

"Is this building all on one level?"

"I'm sorry?"

"Do you have a basement? A cellar? Something under the ground?"

"I... no—"

"Steps leading down from here?"

She looked at Svelt's desperate eyes with concern.
"Are you alright, sir?"
"Yes. I'm sorry, just a bit tired, that's all."
"There's only one staircase in this building, which leads to our living quarters on the first floor. May I ask why you want to know?"
"Have you seen these symbols before? Anywhere in the building?" Svelt asked, showing her the marker and completely ignoring her question.
"No, never."
She shook her head nervously, feeling threatened by the troll's interrogating manner. Svelt placed some coins on the counter and headed for the door.
"Thank you," he said wearily.
"Sir! Your bakes!"
The Flamin' Bun sat on the corner of a small square surrounded by houses and several other shops. An alleyway ran alongside the bakery and appeared to be the only access to the rear of it, where a small courtyard backed up to the old building, but all sides were walled.

Now, where?

Even if the little yard contained hidden secrets, there was no visible means of entry. He walked along the backstreet alleyway—moving away from the bakery—with his lumpy shoulders slumped, kicking a stone out of pure frustration. It bounced a short way along the alley before disappearing. Arriving where it had mysteriously vanished, the reason soon became apparent—a metal grate had been let into the cobblestones.

Kneeling on the ground and peering through it didn't reveal anything in the darkness below, but he sensed the presence of great depth. The sound of flowing water could be heard very faintly. He dropped another stone through the grate. A short silence followed before the *splash* of stone hitting water reached him. Svelt wasn't sure how this was helping, but as he got up, he noticed something. To the left of the grate, chiselled into the stone, was a tiny symbol! It was insignificant in terms of the map, but he remembered it from an old book. Three curvy lines stacked on top of each other. *Water*.

Svelt looked around frantically until he spotted another grate further along the alleyway. Moving quickly towards it, he immediately checked the cobblestones to the side. Another symbol, but again, not what he was expecting. A simple stick arrow had been chiselled into the stone. It was pointing towards the wall of a building, or, if you viewed it from the same perspective as the water symbol, it was possibly pointing forward.

Svelt ran to the next grate, where he was almost relieved to find a triangle! He knelt and dropped a stone through one of the slots. The lengthy silence offered two possibilities. A bottomless pit, or the far more likely explanation of the stone landing on something soft. Moving briskly and scanning the ground excitedly for another symbol led to further disappointment and frustration. No more grates in the cobblestones. A little further ahead, the alleyway was crossed by a low stone wall, with no buildings visible in the distance. A dead end. He slowly walked towards the wall, feeling exhausted and deflated. When he reached it, Svelt was pleasantly surprised to see the river some way off. It lifted his spirits slightly. He expected a bank wall to be higher but soon realised it was merely an inset parapet, with the barrier's edge being a few steps away on the other side and then a long drop to the shore below. Turning around, he leaned against it and looked back along the alley.

To his left, the side of one of the buildings backed almost against the wall, leaving a small gap. To his right were a few trees, bushes, and a tangle of thorns and weeds. Svelt noticed the weeds had formed into a rounded hillock within the undergrowth, and as he ventured over, he realised it was mostly ivy leaves. He fought his way through the overhanging branches and thorns before stopping at the mound of vegetation.

Ivy clings and climbs. It has no backbone to grow upwards of its own accord.

As he began to strip it away in long strands, his hand hit something solid... something *metal*.

Tearing larger clumps of ivy from the mound revealed more metal. Once the remaining stalks had been cleared from the edges, he stood back to grasp a clearer picture of the object he'd uncovered. A large dome of thin iron latticework—unquestionably old and set into an oval of stone. For all the world, it looked just like an eye!

Svelt looked through the bars of the dome into the depths below and could barely make out the outlines of what appeared to be a winding stone stairway. It was very dark.

Zeqar had a dilemma. He could kill the creature right there, and that would be an end to it. But his disappearance would surely alert those following events, and others, *significant* others, would come. He was standing in the shadows of the alleyway, watching Svelt peer into the eye. Alternatively, he could take the map from the creature, and it would be free to live its life unharmed—in body, at least. But then, as well as knowledge of the map, it would also hold memories of this place, tormenting its mind, forcing it to return. A third option remained. He could let the creature find the artefact in full view of the observer, which would lead the time-meddler to believe he'd accomplished his goal. Once the interfering monkey was out of the way and the creature emerged from the eye, he could kill it before any damage was done—snuffing out the image in its mind before destroying the map, too. Zeqar smiled and leaned back against the wall.

Svelt searched around the skirt of metalwork for a hinge or lock but found it was devoid of any such mechanisms—obviously never intended as an entrance or exit, merely placed there as a somewhat intricate seal. He tugged hard at the bars, and a few tiny cracks appeared around the fixing points. Tugging again loosened small stone chips. A third time forced the structure to give. After several more attempts, he had bent it enough to allow for squeezing inside. Before attempting to, he gathered the loose brambles and ivy into a bundle next to the opening. Svelt took the plunge. Standing at the top of the stairway, reaching through the bars, he pulled most of the foliage over the dome. Nauseating darkness followed, oblivious to the dappled, patchy light. Sidling against the back wall of the cylindrical stairway, he edged his way cautiously down the steps…

Breakthroughs

Percy had the attention of the whole bar. Even a colossal block of marble was capable of higher concentration levels than an inn full of trolls.

"Look, it very simple. Tonight, Svelt bringin' 'is girlfriend 'ere."

"Yeah, so wot de problem den?" asked an even less coherent Bam, who was still suffering from the previous night's antics despite a morning of trying to drink himself sober.

"I told you, she not a troll."

"Neeva is Svelt, really," laughed Blok, who had only met him the night before.

"Less of dat, please, Svelt a good guy," warned Percy.

"Well, to be 'onist, Percy, *you* ain't ig-zak-lee de full tick—"

"Say one more word, an' I'll smash your teef in!"

"I woz jus' sayin'," explained Rom.

"Well, don't!"

"So, wot de problem wiv dis girl den?" repeated Bam.

Percy stared at the collection of blank, puzzled faces and couldn't hold it in any longer.

"Look, there *is* no problem—she is merely a different species but also happens to be elegant and perfectly beautiful... understand!"

The trolls looked around at each other.

"Whad 'e jus' say?"

"Ain't got a clue, 'e went all weird. Go an' knock some troll into 'im."

Rom strode up to the bar, and his massive fist came down on the top of Percy's head, who duly collapsed in a rocky heap.

"Betta?" asked Rom.

Percy's hand appeared above the bar by way of submission. "B-betta... much b-betta, f-fanks."

*****

In response to new developments, Chief Lopez had requested an entire division of the bravest, most vigilant officers Landos had to offer. But he had to settle for the herd now standing before him instead.

"Gentlemen, we have a breakthrough at last! Our man was spotted leaving *Church de Noted Dame* a little earlier. If you happen upon him, you have my permission to arrest on the spot. Try not to take that literally, Fred. The kitty won't survive another medi-cart bill. But everyone, *please* remember not to be fooled by his appearance."

"*And* rough him up a bit, sir?"

"What?"

"Rough him up. Do we have your permission for that, too?"

"We are professionals, Tombs. I know you are new and keen, but that's not how we perform our public duties."

"Sorry, sir. It's just... I heard you say you would like to kill the bastard yourself. So, I didn't think you'd object to a little elbow *here*, or maybe a knee to the essentials... *perhaps*? Just to be getting on with."

Attempted snigger suppression followed among the officers.

"I was just thinking out loud, Tombs. I didn't actually *mean* it."

"Sorry, sir."

"Right. Bert will—"

"But... he *did* kill two people, sir."

Lopez looked at the colossal officer thoughtfully. In the dark, if only his outline was visible, he could easily be mistaken for a troll. His face was a picture of caged enthusiasm just bursting to get out. "Okay, Tombs... a bit."

"Thank you, sir."

"But don't overdo it."

"No, sir. Of course not."

"Right! Bert will brief you on your sweep locations while Frank and I search for someone else..." Lopez paused briefly as a concerned look crossed his face, "...someone who needs our protection. We shall cover the west side. Be careful, gentlemen, this— oh, sorry... *and* Tombs—this guy is a murderer. Dismissed."

The officers started filing out of the station.

"Dabble, Trubble, come here, please."

The patrons of poltroonery slowly walked towards the chief with their heads hung low.

"Well done, boys! Due to your tireless efforts with Eddi's sketches, we have a sighting."

"Well, actually, sir—" a lightning-quick boot to the shin cut short the damage potential of Barny's intended sentence. "Owww!" he cried, rubbing his leg.

Fred's limbs were dormant for much of the time, but when the need arose, he had surprisingly quick reactions for a grossly rotund man. For some reason, which only ear-to-brain instant recognition analysis understood, they only 'kicked in' when Barny's mouth was about to get them placed on mucking out duties again.

"Cramp again, Barny?"

"Old war wound, sir."

"There hasn't been a war in your entire, pointless lifetime!"

"That's why it's old, sir, s'bin passed down through generations."

"Was idleness present in your ancestors too?"

"Oh *yes*, sir. The Trubbles 'ave been admired an' worshipped by all down the years." Fred nodded and stared directly ahead as Barny continued. "You might 'ave 'eard the famous sayin', sir… Stand! 'ere comes Trubble."

"I think you're confusing 'idle' with 'idol', 'stand' with 'hide', and historical fact with dreams, Barny. Off you go then."

Fred saluted. "Fank you, sir."

"Yes, sir," said Barny.

The chief watched them walk away, shook his head, and reached for his coat.

"Sir?"

"Yes, Frank."

"What do you suppose our fugitive was doing in Cheese Square?"

"I know what you're thinking… Church de Noted Dame is not your usual place of worship. Then again, I'm not entirely sure our priest is a priest. Let's go and find out, shall we?"

The large frame of Fred and the almost dwarf-like form of Barny—still limping slightly—started off down the street, side by side.

"Fred?"
"Yeah?"
"Feel a bit guilty now."
"Wot for?"
"Dumpin' all them pictures in the river."

*****

Brutus Stratus had a very keen eye for the smallest of details. He instantly noticed the hasty repositioning of the wooden pieces on the pry-minister's stressboard.

"How are you getting on, sir?"

"Very well, thank you, Brutus. I've been painstakingly perfecting a ruthless, killer move," Victor said, tapping the side of his nose.

"Excellent! When you feel ready, I would be honoured to be your first opponent."

"All in good time, Brutus, all in good time. More news?"

"Indeed, yes, sir. Most exciting, too! We have more information on the clever chap who came up with the 'River Guard' idea."

"Really? Who is it?"

"His name is Svelt Hamfist."

"That's a strange name."

"He is a troll *of sorts*. In fact, the son of a troll and a dwarf. I believe he was treated very harshly as an infant, but he obviously has no ill feelings towards authority. He loves and cares deeply about the city."

"He must be rewarded, Brutus."

"Exactly what I was thinking, sir."

"A medal, perhaps?" the pry-minister suggested.

Brutus gave a politely exaggerated cough.

"I was thinking more along the lines of a place on the committee. Mr Hamfist is undoubtedly intelligent, forward-thinking, and understands both dwarves and trolls alike. In fact, from what I hear, he's not doing too badly on *other* fronts, either. Our friend is also young and in touch with the world—in stark contrast to certain members currently in office." Brutus took a deep breath. "He could be, dare I say it, the first non-privileged member in the committee's history!"

"Is that a good thing, Brutus?"

"Just think. The caring pry-minister makes amends for the previous ill-treatment of this unfortunate fellow by giving him a place on the committee. It would be very popular with the pub—everyday man on the street, sir. Somebody on the inside, fighting for their rights, etc."

"Yes, of course. People might start to like me."

"Well... *over time*, perhaps, but it would certainly be a start."

"I'm not sure the other members would be too happy about it. Don't they have to vote him in?"

"Usually, sir, yes. That's where you come in. As pry-minister, you can override any vote or proposal—this would be by Rule Appointment!" Brutus threw his arms open theatrically.

"Yes, I could, couldn't I?"

"Of course, sir."

"Brutus, it's not just because he's a troll... is it?"

"Perish the thought!"

"Very well. If you would be so kind as to draw up—"

Brutus produced a parchment, seemingly from nowhere.

"I have already taken the liberty, sir. Hope you don't mind?"

"My, that was quick."

Victor signed the parchment.

"I shall inform the committee immediately and begin the search for Svelt Hamfist!" cried Brutus as he almost *ran* to the door.

Victor watched the door close and waited for the footsteps to get fainter… he wasn't sure that would happen any time soon, but judging by the crunching sound, he knew the deputy was crossing the courtyard. Satisfied the required distance had been reached, he hurled the stressboard across the floor with all his might. Some pieces stayed 'onboard', surfing the tiles impressively until they hit the wall.

"Stupid game, anyway. And what *idiot* named it *stress*!"

*****

"Shall we take a shortcut to Old Town, Fred?"

"Nah, not down there, Barny."

"Why not?"

"It's creepy… look at the sign."

Barny looked up. "Definit Lee. Wot's *lee* mean?"

"I've 'eard 'em say it at the docks before, fink it means shelter."

"*That* is an old alley, not a shelter."

"Nah, I mean, like, shelter from the wind an' rain."

"Oh, right. Well, that sounds all right then."

"First of all, it's summer. Secondly, even if it weren't, I *still* wouldn't go down *there*."

"Can't be that bad."

"I'm telling you, it's creepy. The shops are never open."

"What?"

"The shops, Barny. They are obviously tended to and occupied, but they are never open. The 'closed' signs are always up."

"Don't be silly, there must—"

"I've only bin down there twice... never again."

"C'mon, I'll prove there's nuffin' to worry about. Assumin' you can fit, o' course."

"Oh, *ha-ha*. You'll be sorry, pal."

They entered the ridiculously narrow alleyway. The timber buildings seemed to lean forward and almost touch rooftops, making it unnaturally dark and gloomy. The first two shops they passed were indeed closed.

Barny started whistling an erratic tune. Slightly louder than necessary. "Probably on their lunch break, eh?"

"I don't fink so, Barny... it's way past that time."

"Look, there's a butcher's shop. Now *that* can't be permanently closed, can it?"

They edged closer to the window and peered in, where, sure enough, a bountiful display of freshly cut meat had been neatly arranged inside wooden trays.

"See."

"Yeah, but the door's still locked, an' there's no sign o' life inside."

"Okay, Fred, point taken... let's go!"

At exactly halfway along the lee, dead centre of the cobblestone road, a perfect marble sphere sat atop a stone pillar. The word '... open' had been chiselled into it. They looked at each other and checked the other side, which was identical. '... open'.

"... open? *Wot's*... open?"

"I don't know, but I ain't waitin' to find out."

"Me neither."

The officers hurried along the road towards the daylight further ahead. Barny moved decidedly quicker when he noticed *Lily Black*—a shop displaying venomous-looking blooms—and an ancient tavern named *Whet ye Tonge*. A lost, parched, exhausted desert trekker wouldn't have ventured into it, even if he wasn't hallucinating. They were all dead silent and bereft of any activity.

They reached the light of the adjoining road and breathed a double sigh of relief. Barny turned swiftly, half-expecting to see somebody creeping up on them... nothing. Then he noticed the sign.

" 'ere, Fred."

"Wot?"

"I thought this road was called Definit Lee."

"It is."

"Not this end, it ain't."

Fred lifted his eyes slowly to the sign on the corner of the building. "Eturn Lee. *Eturn Lee*? C'mon, Barny, let's get well away from 'ere."

"Shortcut it may be, but you were right, Fred. I could do wiv the exercise, know wot I mean?"

"Well, that's where you an' me are different, see. I, meself, am a natural athlete, 'cos I always take the longest route to anywhere involving work."

"Yeah, but you don't run there."

As the duo embarked on a swifter-than-usual walk towards Old Town, a black cat watched them with interest until they were beyond sight. She then turned her attention back to Eturn Lee, where a tall, hooded figure dressed entirely in black staggered from the alley. He was using a fearsome agricultural tool as a walking aid while clutching a small brown parcel tied with string under his arm. The scruffy feline sniffed the air hungrily and began to follow the unmistakable aroma of freshly butchered meat drifting from the paper bundle. Death stopped at the junction, swaying and flickering slightly, seemed to get his bearings and tottered off along the road, hiccupping... before disappearing into thin air.

Revelations

In darkness, even the simplest of passages can feel treacherous. Stairs are particularly tricky, especially when the stone risers are inconsistent. Svelt's head swam. An ancient well missing the original centrepiece, now threatening the unseen presence of emptiness and a long drop. The spiralling steps clung precariously to the wall, and he hoped they continued to the bottom.

He wouldn't know until it was too late.

As he slowly descended, it was so deadly quiet that the sound of his breathing was making him panic, which in turn was making him breathe more rapidly. Fearing his heart would pound through his chest at any moment, the thumping beat was almost deafening in contrast to the silence around him.

After what seemed like hours, Svelt's eyes began to embrace the shadowy surroundings. There didn't appear to be any light below, but as he edged further down, the faint outline of the next step became visible—he hoped he wasn't hallucinating. Doubting himself for the briefest moment, he continued warily, and gradually, the outlines became clearer. Progress was quicker now, and he moved much more freely with the comfort of knowing what was beneath his feet. After negotiating what seemed like another hundred steps, he couldn't make out the edge of the next one, and the darkness seemed to flood back in around him—he stopped. Dangling his foot tentatively over the edge, he lowered it slowly, petrified of over-balancing and plunging to his death. A jolt to the bottom of his foot jarred his leg, but the slight give in the surface told him he had reached the bottom. He planted the other foot beside it.

An exploratory hand to the right and his fingers met a cold, damp surface. It was the same in front. After a turn to the left, Svelt realised he was standing in a narrow corridor, the walls of which were solid stone for as far as he could see, but the floor was soft. Even with the limitations of his unyielding touch, he knew it was sand. He knelt, scooped a handful, and let the grains slip through his fingers like a sparkling waterfall. Looking along the sandy carpet at the only way forward, he stood again and made for the end wall. A tiny amount of light from somewhere up ahead barely illuminated a corner, which turned to the right.

He approached it with extreme caution, listening intently for any sound, but even if somebody did jump out on him, there was nowhere to turn. Peering around the corner revealed another slightly longer corridor, where the light gradually improved towards the end. Seeing nothing to hinder his progress, Svelt proceeded slowly but soon realised his eyes had deceived him. He approached the previously unseen obstacle, which presented a decidedly *tangible* challenge. No more corners and no way forward. A dead end.

The walls on either side were made of stone, but straight ahead, tiny gaps allowed stronger light to filter through. With hands outstretched, Svelt shuffled to the end wall where, much to his surprise, it wasn't stone he encountered but wooden slats—too tightly fitted to reveal anything beyond.

With the corridor barricaded from behind, he took the only option and shoulder barged the tinder-dry timber aside as though it were paper. The unexpectedly wide-open space offered extra light, which was most welcome. A fair way into the distance, two torches hung on the wall, one on either side of a strange-looking portal. High above, a roughly rectangular opening allowed daylight to filter in, and glancing over to the ground beneath, he spotted some debris. He ventured over to the strewn objects, standing directly under the source of light way up in the vast ceiling of the chamber. On the ground at his feet were two thick wooden beams with holes at either end, indicating they had once been attached to something. Lengths of splintered wood also lay scattered around. Examining one of the fragmented pieces suggested it was part of an old floorboard.

Svelt dropped the wood and set off towards the torches at the far end of the sand-covered expanse. Approximately halfway across, he noticed another doorway to his left-hand side and changed direction to investigate. On closer inspection, he found it to be a standard wooden door. It was locked. Peering through the keyhole revealed a wide staircase just beyond a small hallway. The outer door frame was made of large stone blocks and appeared much older than the wooden inner—it also bore some strange markings. He continued towards the torches. The entrance between them was an unusual shape—more of a pentagon than a rectangle—built with stone blocks of a similar age to those he'd just seen. The two familiar symbols, triangle and eye, were engraved above it, but he noticed they were not circled by a silver ring on this occasion. A curtained rail had been fixed between the two straight jambs as a substitute for the missing solid door, leaving a small triangle of space above.

The sputtering torches warmed him as he slid the curtains aside, and, taking a deep breath, Svelt entered the unknown…

*****

Patrolling the busier areas adjacent to Old Town now seemed vastly more appealing than strange dark alleyways—shortcut or not—where two of the city's finest upholders of law might expect welcoming praise and adoration from local traders and the general public. Fred and Barny, on the other hand, soon found themselves ambling around a rapidly emptying forum.

"S'bin a warm day, Fred, but I fink it might rain later."

"Yeah, reckon so."

"Funny ol' business wiv this priest bloke."

"Sure is, pal. Nasty piece o' work."

"Fred?"

"Yeah?"

"Are *you* religious?"

"Well, me ol' mum did insist on takin' me to church every weekend."

"Did she? Bit much to take in when you're a kid, eh?"

"*Yeah… yeah…* but I was forty-nine last time she dragged me there, Lord rest 'er soul… *please*?"

"Well, that's gotta count then, ain't it?"

"I s'pose, but to be 'onist, I still couldn't get me 'ead around all that 'Thou shalt not this' an' Thou shalt not that', if you know wot I mean."

"No. Wot does 'shalt not' mean?"

"It means, shall not, or shouldn't."

"Shall not? Wot, like telling you wot to do?"

"Well, not telling, as such, just politely reminding you of wot's right and wrong."

"Give us an example then."

"Okay," said Fred. "Thou shalt not steal."

"Steal? Oh, you mean like… nick an 'orse, or sumfin' like that?"

"Stealing is stealing. Could be an apple off a stall… s'all the same, y'know."

"*Is it?*" asked Barny, a little surprised.

"Oh yeah. Then there's 'Thou shalt not cavort thy neighbour's wife'. Very naughty that one."

"Wassat mean? Cavort?"

"Basically, it's warning you not to 'ave relations wiv another man's wife. In your case, that also includes 'leering at' for a bit longer than a glance should take."

"Yeah, but it's alright though, 'cos she lives in the next street."

"Doesn't matter."

"Don't it? Oh dear," replied Barny, getting a little bit concerned. "Yeah, but 'e can't be everywhere at once, can 'e?"

" 'oo can't?"

"Y'know… 'im!" said Barny, gesturing upwards with his eyes. "The good lord."

"Don't be so sure, pal, 'cos it depends on wot you believe. Strange forces are at work."

"Bloody 'ell! Well, wot 'appens to blokes that break them rules then?"

"Oh, nuffin' much. I wouldn't worry about it."

"Oh, you 'ad me going there, Fred. Thought I woz in trouble."

"Nah, mate, nah. Rule-breakin' blokes, much like yerself, just spend all eternity being tortured wiv instruments of Satin."

"Well, that don't sound *too* bad…"

" 'ang on, that's not right. Oh yeah, that's it. Not Satin… *Satan*! Instruments of *Satan*!"

"What!"

"Oh, an' I forgot the bit about the pit o' fire."

"Fred?"

"Yes, Barny?"

"Fink I'm toast."

*****

…which turned out to be a small cave! A tingling sensation washed over Svelt as he surveyed his new surroundings amidst the flickering glow granted by the light of a single torch. It was a luxury he savoured after his recent brushes with darkness. His eyes were immediately drawn to shadowy recesses cut from the bare rock, containing several large stone tablets. He moved closer. The tablets were covered in small symbols and pictures, either carved *into* or applied *to* the stone. He ran his fingers over one of them, feeling the slightly raised image. To a troll, they could be considered a rather macabre example of cutaneous bibliopegy, in this case, the skin binding being stone. To a *dwarf troll*, they were still beautiful.

The wall beside the stone 'bookcase' was covered with posturing stick characters forming a great tale. Svelt tried to decipher the pictures and piece the story together, although he wasn't sure which image announced the beginning and which marked the end. However viewed, it began with a stone bookcase, like the one next to him, and ended with one. The pictures told of an epic voyage; a land of huge, triangular buildings appeared at what he now assumed to be the beginning. Many men carried solid tablets of stone across deserts, oceans, and fields, then continued their labour by constructing temples worthy of displaying them. One of which he now happened to be standing in. He touched the ancient bookcase, and a shudder ran through his body—the ghosts of ages, sacrifice, and great suffering. The desire to share knowledge had taken monumental efforts.

He looked deeper into the cave and spotted a black curtain covering what he assumed was another room. An aura of light surrounded it. Many objects were lying around—some very old, but others were everyday items.

Svelt cautiously approached the curtain and felt a stream of air beyond it. He braced himself. Pulling it swiftly to one side did not prepare him for what lay beyond... a room full of natural light! His eyes were not yet acclimatised enough to bear such an assault, and he turned away. Trying again, he looked up to the source but struggled to keep his eyes open as the light was being reflected by countless pieces of mirror-like glass. The narrow shaft continued upwards, way beyond sight.

Just above the ceiling level of the cave, hidden by the light blazing downwards, Shajar-wah perched on a recessed ledge.

The redirected beam terminated at a stone plinth, illuminating it spectacularly, and Svelt stared blankly at the object placed upon it.

He had found the artefact.

*****

A scream rang out.

"Officers, come quickly. My friend has been robbed!"

A large hand grabbed Barny's arm.

"Don't you worry, madam, my little colleague 'ere will—"

Fred was distracted by a bald-headed man wearing strange robes. He was standing across the square from them.

"Fred… 'elp!" Barny was 'led' away, face etched with fear, by two stout women.

Fred whistled tunelessly and began a feigned 'amble' across the square. After a few yards, he picked up his pace slightly, hoping the man hadn't seen him. Unfortunately for Fred, Zeqar had spotted him and turned slowly, walking in the opposite direction back towards the alleyway he had appeared from. Fred lurched into a plodding run, trying hard to keep his balance, while Zeqar quickened his pace and entered the alleyway. The flagging officer attempted to break into a sprint, but those days were long gone. He jogged along and alerted any nearby officers with his whistle instead—at least, that was the idea. But whistles are far more effective when you force air into them rather than sucking it out in desperate gulps. The holy man was much quicker than him but appeared to have run into a dead end.

He turned and faced Fred with his back to the low wall, giving him the most evil-looking grin the officer had ever seen. Fred was a big man, but sadly, most of it was sideways—he was scared. He edged towards the bald man and tried to blow his whistle again. Zeqar felt the officer had got close *enough* and smiled before falling backwards over the wall. Fred didn't know whether to laugh or cry as he cautiously approached the barrier, half-expecting a trap. He certainly wasn't laughing when he looked down to the ground way below, expecting to see the sprawled body of the priest lying there. What he *saw...* was *nothing*.

The spooked lawman gazed reflectively out to the river, then up to the sky above.

"Well, I'll be burgered."

*****

After another fruitless search, Chief Lopez rested against the bank wall to ponder before his reluctant return to the station. He looked down at the murky grey substance barely fitting the description of 'a river'.

I don't know where you are, Mr Hamfist, but you were right about one thing. It may not be pretty, but it certainly has an indistinct character all of its own.

As he turned to leave, something caught his eye. Washed up on the narrow shore, a vaguely familiar object. After walking to the nearest gap in the wall, he made his way back along the water's edge to investigate. Lopez untied the knot and peered inside, only to be rewarded with the shock of his life... Zeqar's face stared back at him with a mocking grin. Not once, but dozens of times. He turned the sack upside down, and a pot fell into the mud at his feet. A pot containing something utterly dissimilar to glue.

"Those dodgy, *lazy*, useless little f— I'll bloody kill 'em!"

Later that day, a somewhat bewildered officer entered The City Law Station in a daze.

"If I were you, Fred, I'd disappear for a while. The chief's in a foul mood."

"Hah! Disappear… that's very funny, Bert."

"Eh? Are you alright, Fred?"

"Er… I… I…"

"Oh dear, too late."

"DABBLE! Get in here… NOW!"

"Y-yes, sir."

Fred closed the door behind him.

"What the hell do you think you two were d—"

"I found 'im, sir."

"What?"

"Zeqar, sir… I found 'im."

"Zeqar! Where is he then?"

"Gone."

"What do you mean g— have you been drinking again, Dabble?"

"Absolutely not, sir," Fred replied truthfully.

"So, what happened?"

"He flipped over the wall and disappeared, sir."

"I'm in no mood for games, Dabble. I will suspend you with no pay if you don't give me an acceptable explanation. In fact, forget that. Considering your *revised* efforts with the wanted posters, I'll damn well *arrest* you for neglect of duties, criminal damage, and bloody PEE-LOOSE-ON! Now I ask you again. *What… happened?*"

"I cornered him in an alleyway, sir, and… and he… disappeared."

Lopez stared at Fred and knew something wasn't right.

"Fred, this man is a murderer. We desperately need to catch him and throw away the key. You had a golden opportunity to bring him in, and he *DISAPPEARS*!" The chief was purple with anger, which was an impressive feat, given his natural appearance.

"Sir, I—"

Lopez realised Fred was shaken by *whatever* had happened, but more to the point, he didn't trust himself not to do something regrettable. *Violently* regrettable. His large palm covered furrowed brow and closed eyes.

"Fred, go home. We'll speak again tomorrow when things have calmed down."

"Yes, sir. Thank you, sir."

Fred was about to leave when two officers barged in, carrying Barny on a stretcher.

"Fred..." he moaned.

"Barny! Wot 'appened? Did you catch the robber?"

"There *was* no robber, Fred. Jus' a bunch of wimmin wot like muscular men in uniform. It's 'appening, Fred, I'm paying for all me sins."

"Barny, I don't fink it's that."

The chief's mood lightened slightly, seeing Barny's stricken expression. It *almost* made him break into a smile.

"It woz 'orrible, Fred, 'orrible wot they did to me."

"Barny... I..."

The chief couldn't hold out any longer. "Frank!"

"Yes, sir?"

"I want these women found and arrested."

"What's the charge, sir?"

"Calling Barny *muscular*."

Frank and the chief burst into laughter.

"Fred…"

Barny's whimpering voice faded as he was carried off along the corridor.

Despite the combined efforts of the church and his mum over the long years, Fred had taken a major step towards enlightenment.

Make Ends Meet

"What... *is it?*"

Svelt's brain simply couldn't take in the visual information. Standing before him was a square wooden box, the front of which was mostly taken up by a window of grey glass. Just to the right side, four protruding stalks were aligned in a column below a large disc. Two metal spikes embedded into a small dome sat on top, which reminded him of antlers or twig-thin rabbit ears.

Svelt summoned up enough courage to touch the top surface. At first sight, he had assumed it was made of wood, but the feel of the smooth, shiny finish proved otherwise because the knots and grain appeared to have been somehow 'painted' on. Now closer, the low hum in the background that had gone unnoticed on entry grabbed his attention. Behind the strange object, he found the source—a smaller box made of an unusual material he had never encountered before. Two thin ropes streamed from it and led into the back of the artefact. He tried tentatively to touch one of the ropes, but the humming got louder, and the surrounding air began to crackle with an unseen power. Svelt pulled his hand away. He didn't know why, but it reminded him of a mother feeding her baby, except the nutrients seemed to be coming from the *small* box.

Moving to the front again, he carefully pushed one of the stalks, which retracted with a *click*. Trying another produced the same result but caused the first to pop back out. He quickly tried the disc in anticipation, but it didn't move.

"Maybe I have to pull—"

it came off in his hand! He was distraught and started to panic. Looking frantically at the disc, then at the short white stalk it had left behind, he pushed it back on, where, to his utter relief, it stayed put.

The disc was four times the diameter of the stalks but didn't protrude anywhere near as far. With that in mind, he approached it again and tried to turn it instead; an audible *click* followed by a loud crackling sound confirmed that he had set *something* in motion. Svelt began to edge slowly away as the window burst into life, filling with *light*! The bewildered troll fell backwards with a cry and almost fled the cave, fearing he'd be snared by some evil, unnatural force, but then he stopped and looked back. It didn't seem harmful, more like a display of benign magic. Where before the glass had been grey, now, it was alive with hundreds of tiny inky specks dancing around like flies in a jar. Svelt found it *so* mesmerising that he could have watched it forever. He edged closer again, and something strange happened. Faint outlines were now visible and moved around in the back of the window.

"There must be a way in."

Upon examining the rear for a small door or hidden hinges, he found a row of thin slots running along the top. He peered through them, directly into the box innards, but what he saw did not register. Hundreds of tiny metal blobs alongside tubes and many other strange shapes. He had seen nothing like it before but was still disappointed to find the interior was clearly devoid of little people. Turning his attention back to the outside of the mystical device, Svelt gingerly touched one of the spikes, which prompted a louder crackling sound and caused odd stinging sensations in his hand. Without really knowing why he did it, he moved the spikes apart slightly and looked at the window again. To his amazement, the outlines had changed. They were still unclear, but for a fraction of a second, he was sure he'd seen a face!

The magic box was incredible, but it also scared him a little. Approaching the disc again, unable to resist, the fascinated troll twisted it, producing a horrendous roaring sound. He scrabbled furiously at the disc, turning it back the other way until... *click*! The window faded and returned to its original flat-grey colour.

Svelt didn't know what to do next. He had no idea what he was looking at or the box's purpose.

What would the wizard have done with this? Am I supposed to take it? Surely not. It's too big and awkward.

Shajar-wah was becoming a little impatient.

Can the creature take this unique opportunity any further? It has, after all, shown impressive stamina to get this far.

Svelt looked around, and an idea came to him. Picking up a piece of parchment and quill that happened to be lying on the floor, he began to draw the box in as much detail as possible. Only words could capture his experience and feelings, but at least he could recreate the visuals. After numerous attempts and now satisfied with his best effort, he reluctantly left the cave. Neatly folding the parchment, he tucked it into his pouch.

Immediately after Svelt's departure, Shajar-wah dropped to the floor and aimed a craggy stick at the box—it vanished in a flash of light. Halos of white fire surrounded his hands as he effortlessly lifted a large stone tablet from the ground. He brushed the sand away and returned it to its usual resting place. Once more, the immense book sat proudly on its raised plinth, illuminated by a glorious beam of golden light. Shajar-wah the Observant watched Svelt trudge away across the sand and felt *slightly* disappointed. His instincts urged him to follow the troll and oversee the outcome, but in his resurrected form, he was confined to boundaries that, if broken, could prove disastrous. With the task hopefully complete—albeit with some unexpected developments—he headed purposefully towards the stone tablets. Which, of course, sat in one of the oldest libraries on the planet.

Svelt was deeply puzzled but felt he had done what was expected of him. He'd heard of a place called The School of Miserable Tricksters and briefly contemplated visiting the great castle to inform them of the discovery, until the face of the dying wizard floated back into his mind, and he realised the knowledge he now possessed was deadly. With a shudder, he wondered if the killer would still be looking for *him*.

With this thought gnawing at him, Svelt stopped suddenly halfway across the antechamber. Fearing the winding stair, he headed instead for the door. He hoped it was now unlocked, but ultimately, that would have led to him receiving unwanted visitors during his mystifying discovery. Trying the handle again, only one option remained, and he obliterated the door. The relieved troll was happy to find the stairs were even, with the added luxury of a landing above each flight.

When he reached the top, he was surprised by the lack of a conventional exit—just a trap door set into the ceiling. A large wooden crate sat beneath it, which had obviously been placed to aid entry or exit. Svelt listened for footsteps or voices above and stood on the edges of the box, which was not as solid as he'd hoped. Praying it would hold out, he pushed the trap door but felt some resistance—a thick rug doubling as the time-honoured method of concealment. Grabbing the sides of the opening, he thrust his body upwards, causing the box to splinter, and dragged himself to the floor above.

To his surprise, he was standing in an office. Glumly sparse in decor, although the two symbols were prominent again. He exited the room into a narrow corridor, passing a small library along the way, straight into a hall—where he had discovered the third marker... he was back in Sant Jon's! Looking over to the pedestal previously displaying the book, he noticed a few chairs had been placed around the area in front of it. The reason soon became apparent—several boards were missing, leaving a large hole in the floor. He stared at the opening, recalling his narrow escape from a plunge into blackness, and slid outside into the hazy evening.

Checking every corner, Svelt suddenly became aware of potential dangers lurking at every turn. He crossed to a nearby tavern and sat alone with his thoughts.

Officer Grunt cursed his luck. He placed his drink on the table and slipped quietly out of the tavern while trying to avoid eye contact with the newcomer, before heading straight for the station.

Following another brief reassessment, the anxious troll tried to convince himself that his crude attempt at capturing the artefact on parchment was *passable* in detail but was still none the wiser to its purpose. The burden of knowledge and the pressure of choosing at least one worthy recipient was already weighing heavy, and even though the wizard's millstone was now shared, he assumed the old timer had already known who to pass the map to before he was waylaid, which was an advantage Svelt didn't have. A stark realisation struck. As of that moment, simply knowing him could be a life-threatening acquaintance.

Time passed…

Svelt stared blankly at his child-like handiwork without realising how long he'd been under its innocent spell. Tearing his eyes away as if snapping out of a trance, he scanned the bar desperately. "Oh no… Vaessa!"

Several people looked over.

"Please, what is the time?" he asked the barman.

"The bell for seven rang out maybe ten minutes back, friend."

"No, no!"

His heart sinking further with every passing minute, Svelt sped towards The Squares, not knowing that Vaessa was still waiting outside the shop.

"What's keeping him?"

Watching her date hurtle around a corner as if being chased by a pack of rabid wolves brought only partial relief.

"Svelt! Where have you been? I was so worried!"

"Vaessa, I'm so sorry," he panted, trying to catch his breath.

"What's happened to you?" she asked, looking at the panic in his eyes.

"You wouldn't believe me if I told you. Please, Vaessa, I'll explain later."

He grabbed her arm, forgetting his strength for a moment, and led her hurriedly towards Westmines.

"Svelt, slow down! What's wrong with you?"

They reached The Cave, the breathless elf still clueless, despite the manic explanations blurted towards her during the frantic trip across town.

"Vaessa, I'm going to leave you here for a while. I have something to do… it won't take long."

"You're not coming in with me?"

"It'll be too complicated… trying to explain everything to them. They will only delay me further."

"Svelt, you're scaring me. Is everything okay?"

"I'm so sorry… please forgive me. Yes, my beautiful bluebell, everything is okay." He cradled the sapphire hanging from her neck. "Ask for Percy. He's expecting us both but will look after you until I return." Svelt paused. "Vaessa, I… I…"

"Tell me when you get back." She kissed him on the cheek. "Svelt, please be careful."

"I will… I promise."

He walked away into the darkening evening.

Vaessa watched him until he was out of sight and entered The Cave alone.

Svelt now understood what needed to be done, but the task could not be carried out in familiar surroundings. He headed away from the centre in a northerly direction and into different territory. There was no need to venture too far, just far *enough*. At last, after almost losing himself, a faint light shone up ahead—a glowing lantern illuminating the sign of a tavern at the end of the street.

"Perfect."

He moved quickly. Before entering the tavern, he noticed a small area of woodland and greenery a short distance beyond.

The Scythe and Pitchfork.

He took it as a good omen—the sign reminded him of home.

He sat at the table, feeling, *hoping* this was the final chapter in the wizard's tale. Trying to avoid unnerving the man upon entry, he'd waited until approaching the bar for another drink before introducing himself to the burly landlord.

"Jed Blake, at your service, sir."

Obviously, several locals were uncomfortable with trolls or dwarves being served at the bar because Svelt sensed a slight air of unrest.

"Jed, can I trust you?"

"Well, I don't even know you, sir, so the question is… can *I* trust *you*?"

"Yes, you are right… sorry. I guess we shall have to trust each other."

Svelt reached into his pouch and handed Jed a lot of coins. "I need you to do something for me."

After a brief conversation, Jed nodded slowly. "Parchman, eh? I don't rightly know whether I trust you *more* or *less* now, sir, but you have my word. It will be done."

"I found this place by chance, Jed, as my path here was a little… erratic. Can you tell me the quickest way back to Westmines?"

"Take the Roseberry Pathway, an old dirt track behind the stables before the orchard gate. It's quicker and straighter than any of the long crescent streets in these parts and leads to cobblestones soon enough."

"Thank you."

The night air felt slightly cooler as Svelt stepped outside but still carried a heavy presence. The unmistakable atmosphere of an approaching storm. Nervously, he ventured into the wooded area, which was very sparsely lit. Ominous shadows threatened everywhere, and the timber buildings seemed to harbour half-hidden figures. Right on cue, after the brief explosion of light, the gentle growl of distant thunder announced the beginning.

After leaving the stables half a mile behind, Svelt reached a rough crossroads on Roseberry Pathway, formed by many passing feet over the years. But tonight, it was desolate. He paused, looking from left to right. Brighter lights and more familiar territory lay ahead in the distance. He spun around to check behind, as if expecting to be followed—the first spots of rain fell, followed by a flash of light and a loud boom.

Abandoning the pathway a short while later allowed his pace to quicken.

He felt decidedly uneasy now, but at least the ground underfoot had returned to reassuring cobblestone. Finally, he approached the first true alleyway, looking further ahead to the intersection and last stretch—

—an unwavering, determined figure sprang from the shadows, rounded the corner purposefully, and stood directly in his path. Pure shock prevented any cry of fright, but Svelt's heart pounded faster than nature had ever intended.

The rain came down harder.

"I know what you have seen."

The tan-skinned man towered above him menacingly. He wore a weather-ravaged robe that had once been white and a small cap on a smooth, bald head.

"Who are you? What do you want?" cried Svelt. He looked into the holy man's eyes. Dark brown in colour, conveying the infinite depth of bottomless pits—ancient and haunted by past horrors.

"My name is not important; I am a messenger of The Lord. You must be made forgetful of this dangerous, unholy glimpse of the future… the knowledge cannot be passed on to others."

"Made forgetful? How can you unsee something? Unknow something?"

"Alas, there is but one way."

"I don't even understand what I've seen and have committed no crime."

The sky boomed overhead as the rain continued to lash them both.

"Enough talk. Give me the map."

"I don't have it anymore."

"I have grown weary of games, and there can be no trail. *Give me the map…* NOW!"

Zeqar pulled a dagger seemingly from nowhere and pointed it threateningly.

"For the last time… the map!"

Svelt attempted to grab the holy man's wrist, but Zeqar was too quick. Spinning swiftly around, he plunged the blade straight into Svelt's side. Much to his horror, it shattered, and the broken pieces disappeared in a flash of white flame. Zeqar screamed with pain as the ancient hilt fell to the ground. He stared at the dwarf troll in disbelief and sensed rare feelings of conflict and indecision from his overseeing master.

The rain came down in torrents, and the sky flashed. Svelt seized his opportunity and charged at

Zeqar, shoulder first, sending the man reeling and landing heavily on his back. Surprised by his own actions, the wary troll backed away slowly.

The thunder boomed again, and the rain fell heavier still.

Zeqar winced and writhed in pain.

"Help me, Lord!" he cried. "He must be punished. He must be stopped. IT WAS YOUR COMMAND!"

The storm drew inwards, and as the rain eased briefly, there seemed to be a pause of uncertain hesitation before the heavens rumbled again. Svelt looked skywards with a feeling of helplessness and foreboding. A globe of light appeared in the blackness above, and erratic streaks of forked lightning arced to the centre. Time seemed to slow…

"Now, Lord… NOW!"

Svelt heard Zeqar's cry, but it sounded deep and distorted, as if underwater. A fog rolled through his mind carrying joyful yet confusing visions…

It's me… I'm a child again! My natural parents— I can see them! There's Old Mother Brown carrying breakfast from the kitchen… Mum and Dad next to the fire in the farmhouse… Vaessa! Don't worry, Vaessa, I won't be long… the artefact—

The present snapped sharply back into focus, and Zeqar continued screaming desperate pleas to the night. The sky turned brilliant white, and a powerful bolt of pure energy arrowed downwards, ripping straight through Svelt's chest, obliterating the ground below him.

Everything stopped. The shouting, the thunder… the rain petered out. Smoke rose from Svelt's lifeless body and the surrounding cobblestones.

Zeqar raised an arm to the sky.

"Thank you, Lord. I am ever your servant!"

He stooped over the small troll. The tunic he wore had no place to conceal anything, but spotting the pouch, he tore it open, and coins spilt onto the ground. He reached tentatively inside, hoping… and then he felt it… *paper*. A rejuvenating rush of relief washed over him as he pulled out the map sections. Zeqar staggered to his feet, wincing with pain again, before offering up the papers in his open palm. They disappeared in a flash of turquoise flame. He turned his hand over and watched the ashes flutter over Svelt's body.

Zeqar retrieved the dagger hilt and started back towards the distant lights, lurching and stumbling as he tried to move faster. Passing the midway point of the alleyway, he looked to the main street just ahead, but he slowed when a large man turned the corner and stood astride the gap. The light behind silhouetted the imposing frame and blacked out his features. Zeqar froze, turned slowly, and started to walk back in the opposite direction. Another figure, slightly smaller but just as menacing, blocked the other junction.

"Good evening, Mr Zeqar!" bellowed Chief Lopez. Inwardly, he was calming the growing rage. "What a pleasant surprise. We are looking for someone… small chap, stony features… perhaps you can help?"

*****

Svelt stood over his former self in a state of confused shock as a swirling mist threatened to engulf him. The veiled outline of a wizard appeared to offer a helping hand on the periphery, but before he could think, feel, or say anything, the greyness was dispersed by a shaft of pure… brilliant… white…

He wasn't sure if he was dreaming, but a voice drifted into his mind.

"Svelt Hamfist, Lord."

"Thank you, Evan. Have you locked up for the night?"

"I… er… *no*, Lord. And there *is* no night or day here."

"Only joking."

"I see. I believe, o great one, you may have used that pun of holy hilarity before… possibly more than once."

"Have I? Is that why you didn't laugh?"

"No."

"Right. Er… that'll be all then."

"My Lord." The gatekeeper bowed and returned to his post.

"Awake, Master Hamfist. You are safe."

The voice wasn't loud, but it seemed to be everywhere. Svelt opened his eyes, but all he could see was white.

"Where am I?"

"Safe from harm, and safe from causing harm."

"W-who are you?"

"I am your maker, your overseer… YOUR LORD!"

The voice boomed around and echoed for an immeasurable amount of time. Svelt fell to the floor and covered his head until it slowly died away.

"But you can call me Gord."

Svelt looked up again.

"Gord?"

"Yes… *Gord*. I am the Lord Gord Almighty. Only the truly wise know my real name, but for some strange reason, many of my flock decided to liken me to a water-carrying bottle made from dried fruit. It's not their fault. It can all get a bit confusing as the centuries roll on."

"Water bottle?"

"Yes. Crazy, isn't it? I can't stand the bloody stuff, either. Doesn't quite hit the spot… if you know what I mean."

"But I have never worshipped any— *you* or even read the holy books."

"What you have, or have not done, does not alter my existence, and lesser beings have also written books. They are not always truthful, though, nor do they have the right to do so, but it is no sin to try and unite people in belief."

"How did I get here? I thought Death—"

"In the end, I required no servant to sever your bodily ties. *I* brought you here."

"Who was that evil man? Why did he kill—"

"Svelt, be silent… *please*. This conflict will rage forever… the advancement of man. Course, they will always strive for more—to do the undoable, reach the unreachable—and there is nothing wrong with that, but! All − in − good − time. When advancement is, erm… *advanced, prematurely*, then… 'Houston, we have a problem.' Hah! Oh, sorry… *ahem*. We have a problem. If these men of science were to realise that every invention, every leap forward, every 'Eureka!' Merely accelerates their own demise…?"

"Then… who made the map?"

"Interferers. From the past."

"Why don't you stop them? As you stopped me?"

"I did, Svelt. Unfortunately, once someone has passed, I have very little control over their actions. Especially when they believe in another… deity. And extra-especially when magic or time is involved. In their early days, they were helped in much the same way they are now trying to pass on to others—wizards are merely a means, a gateway to get their message to the intended people. And they are quite happy to do so, as long as it is a brief involvement and they don't have to get their hands dirty. They have little patience for invention because magic offers a much easier route to their goals, and their time-travelling friends reward them in other ways. Not worshippers, the wizards—they only believe in themselves, but I have to hand it to them... they are a hardy bunch. *Mainly* because they are particularly good at avoiding anything likely to summon my scythe-wielding servant unnecessarily—or, indeed, accidentally."

"So... are you the true lord, sir?"

"I like to think so. Mind you, so do all the others, *including*... er... I'll try and translate into Angless, ahem... The Bun Lord of Triangula. By the way, they've got some things horribly wrong down there, usually where names and words are concerned, but they'll figure it out... eventually. I digress. Svelt, you were a misplaced pawn in a far bigger game, a duel with deadly repercussions for those who stray into the crossfire. I tried to discourage you, warn you, in my own subtle way—"

"The beggar! Why didn't I lis—"

"—but your own pity, remorse and... downright bravery, it must be said, was your undoing. I... I, with great sadness, had to strike you down. Forever."

"I don't understand," cried Svelt.

"That, my son, is the problem."

A tear rolled down Svelt's rough cheek.

"But... but Mum and Dad... Mrs B... Mr Singe... Vaessa... Nooo! I was only beginning to understand true love."

"*True* love? You loved life! And you were also loved in the greatest way of all. You have been most fortunate, my little friend, be thankful for the time spent. You shall see them all again... soon enough."

Svelt hunched into a rocky ball on the floor and wept uncontrollably.

"Svelt. There are two here among us who shall be very glad to receive you into their arms once again. For who you love or fall in love *with* cannot be helped. And neither is it a sin... as long as it is true."

Two shimmering, mismatched figures emerged from the pure white surroundings.

Svelt looked up... and his heart leapt.

Messages

Vaessa waited and waited.

The tears began to flow as she slowly walked to the bar, cradling the sapphire in her hands.

"Bye, Percy... nice to have met you."

Percy was at a complete loss. In the short time he had known Svelt, he would never have envisaged this.

"I am so sorry, my dear. The pleasure was all mine."

Vaessa ran out into the night.

The murmurs and banter began among the trolls.

"Lucky ol' Svelt, eh? Reckon 'e's got *more* boulders on de side."

"Yeah. Hey, Percy, wot you tink about dat den?"

Percy slammed a mug down onto the bar top, causing it to shatter.

"Shut up! I'm really *not* in the mood."

*****

Chief Lopez sat at the table in the confined space of the interrogation room, where he seemed to take up most of it. It's not that he was overweight, but there was simply a lot of him. Opposite sat Zeqar. Manacled behind his back, the chain leading from it ended at Sergeant Frank Moore, who stood astride the door. Not quite as big as the chief, but large *enough* in anyone's book. *Or* door frame, as the case may be. At this moment, the slim, lithe figure of Zeqar resembled the meat in one of Don McCon's bread-heavy offerings.

"Right then, Mr Zeqar—" began the chief.

"Just Zeqar. I have no title."

"I wasn't being *polite*, Mr Zeqar, just menacingly distant. As you have probably gathered by now, you are to be charged with at least two murders. Investigations are ongoing regarding murder number three. Although, I'm reasonably confident the blowpipe you had concealed on your back wasn't ornamental. Do you understand?"

"The troll was struck down by Lord Gord Almighty, sir."

Zeqar said it with the calm assurance of someone telling the absolute truth.

"Did you say… *Gord*?"

"Indeed, yes, sir."

Lopez looked over to Frank, who was shaking his head very slowly. He made a hand gesture to the chief, suggesting Zeqar was mad.

"So, you see, I did not kill the creature."

"Creature?"

Chief Alfonso Lopez was a tough man who had suffered a savage upbringing in the shanties of his hometown. Sadly, Arabica was a country made up entirely of such places, where violence and crime were a way of life. Svelt had been an innocent, honest, likeable chap and, despite his appearance, as harmless as a kitten.

I got there too late.

The thought haunted him for the rest of his life. Not many people got to Chief Lopez, but the despicable charlatan sitting opposite made *him* want to commit murder.

Oh, but you will pay. Make no mistake.

"Creature," he repeated, re-emerging from his thoughts. "The only *creature* that comes to mind is the one sitting opposite me. Okay, Mr Zeqar, let's play it your way. Why did *your Lord* murder Svelt?"

"He is not just *my* Lord, sir. He is *The* Lord, and The Lord does not commit murder. The forbidden knowledge the creature had gained would have caused an irreversible wave of greater sins with far-reaching and dire consequences. Spreading lies, brainwashing people, turning even the faithful away from his word."

He noticed Chief Lopez twiddling the ring on his finger and grinned at him.

"You are an unbeliever, are you not, Mr Lopez?"

"My job requires me to stick to facts, Mr Zeqar. My beliefs require exactly the same."

"But you cannot disbelieve because you have yet to experience something. You are simply in a state of preparation, that is all. The Lord comes to all in some way… eventually. It is just a matter of when it is your time."

The righteous smugness of the man was almost too much to bear, and despite his experience, Lopez couldn't help but retaliate. "I shall rethink my options if, by some miracle, it happens to me."

"Then you shall be a true believer!" smiled Zeqar.

"Grindle Wimp, Mr Zeqar," said the chief, changing the subject.

"I'm sorry?"

"The wizard you murdered… why?"

"Mr Lopez, please stop aiming that word at me. Murder is a sin! Out of mercy, I prevented him from committing terrible sins, for which he would have been punished severely... *forever*. I freed the man!"

"I think Mr Wimp would have preferred a say in matters concerning his freedom."

"Believe me, sir, given a choice, your wizard would remain exactly where he is now rather than a torturous forever with Luc o'fire."

Chief Lopez sighed and leaned back in his chair.

"Mr Zeqar. Do you know the penalty for murder?"

"Yes. Your law states that if you take a life, for whatever reason, you are put to death," recited Zeqar. He did so with pure nonchalance.

"Not *quite*. An unintending soul might kill another person accidentally, even driven by anger or retaliation. There may be mitigating circumstances for which each act is considered individually, but! *Cold-blooded, calculated* MURDER *is* punishable by death!" He relaxed a little. "At least, it is usu—"

"I have faced Death many times, Mr Lopez," interrupted Zeqar, "compared to his usual victims, he found me to be a slightly different proposition."

"I hadn't finished, sir. I was about to say *usually*, but, in your case, I intend to submit a personal recommendation to the pry-minister that *YOU* should spend the rest of your life in The Bridge Tower. I shall personally ensure it is in the smallest, solitary cell therein. As Chief of Law, I think I hold jurisdiction here, so there's no need to put it to the committee. Take this crazy filth away."

"Yes, sir," replied Frank.

As he was led away, Zeqar stopped suddenly, catching the sergeant off guard and jerking him backwards.

"You know, Mr Lopez, your day may come sooner than you think."

Zeqar's maniacal laugh echoed along the corridors as Frank led him away.

Lopez stormed from the interrogation room, strode angrily to his office and slammed the door so hard that his only keepsake tumbled from the shelf onto the floor. He threw his chair out of the way and reached straight into the bottom drawer, pulling out a small glass and a large bottle of golden-coloured liquid from The Heightlands. Only a small amount had been previously consumed—it didn't stay that way for long.

Approximately one month later, the transfer parchments arrived at The City Law Station, signed with approval by the pry-minister and granting permission for Zeqar to be taken to The Tower. During his time under lock and key, the condemned holy-man-cum-lunatic never requested anything. As per regulations, he was given bread and water daily, but the slice remained untouched. Lopez had seen prisoners facing long sentences before, trying to starve themselves, but he wasn't entirely sure it was the case with Zeqar.

"Thought this day would never come."

Chief Lopez allowed himself a small drink by way of celebration.

"Frank! Get Officer Doeball to position the cell wagon as close to the front of the station as possible," called Lopez.

The sergeant appeared at the door.

"Sir, we were supposed to transport two others to the courthouse today. Shall we drop them on the way?"

"No! Mr Zeqar is going all alone. We must eliminate any possible risk—there is to be no contact.

We shall take the shortest route to the river and follow it to The Tower as quickly as conditions allow. Don't want him out of a cell for one second longer than necessary."

"Yes, sir."

Frank left the office and headed to the stables at the rear of the building.

After a short while, Chief Lopez heard the wagon pulling up outside.

"Frank, go and clap him in irons. Take Bert with you."

The officers strode purposefully along the corridor towards the cells.

Lopez closed the office door and waited by the main entrance. He had never experienced the level of absolute hatred towards a criminal that he was feeling right now.

Justice will be done.

An unexpected commotion erupted from the area of the cells, startling Lopez for a second until Frank's raised voice spurred him into action.

"Bastard's finally putting up a fight."

The chief hurried along the corridor.

"Right! *You…*"

Frank headed slowly back towards him, his face whiter than any man's *this* side of the scythe should ever be.

"Frank! What happened? Are you hurt? Where's Bert?"

Frank looked at him in a state of shock and disbelief. "Zeqar's cell is empty… he's *gone*."

To a local onlooker, there was an air of familiarity about the dejected demeanour as Albert Sonny walked, head down, along the path to the lodge he shared with several other students. Unfortunately, he had been demoted from assistant cook to dishwasher in the kitchens where he worked part-time. Again. Meagre as it was, the money was needed to fund his course at The School of Science, which was going surprisingly well. In fact, he was breaking grade records. Eggs and potatoes obviously presented problems of far greater complexity than mere stars and planets ever could.

Two messages were waiting for him in the parch box. One was obviously from the school, but the other bore a seal unknown. He opened the front door, walked along the passageway, and entered his small room. Sitting on the bed, Albert untied the unidentified message, which turned out to be a large piece of age-faded paper. As he unrolled it, a standard-sized writing scroll dropped to the bed.

"What have we here?"

Dear Albert,

I recently went on an adventure and made an incredible discovery. I had no idea what I'd stumbled upon, but knew it must be important, so I tried to draw the strange object. The box came alive with light—it was magical! A crackling sound followed when I moved the thin spikes on top, and very faint images appeared. I'm sure I saw a face in it! Behind it was a smaller box, which seemed to be helping the big one by providing power of some kind. I wish I had your brains.

All the best, friend.

Svelt.

"Svelt!" He hadn't seen his old mate for some time, the last being at *Dogban's Diner* just before the inevitable sacking. He smoothed out the large piece of paper again and studied it with interest. A few minutes passed before something popped into Albert's brain, causing him to spring to life. Grabbing a quill, he dipped it into the inkpot and carefully drew a circle on the left side of the magic box window. He wrote the word 'Bun' inside it. Then, he drew a smaller circle next to it, labelling it 'Loon'. He sat back. "But why would it show motionless objects we can see anyway?" He read through the description again. *'I thought I saw a face in it!'*

Albert turned the parchment over and drew a copy of the box as best he could. He carried it to the window and watched people to-ing and fro-ing busily along the street. Time passed, and inspiration was not forthcoming. As he turned away from the hectic scenes, angry shouts nearby made him look back again.

"Come 'ere, you mangy, thievin' little furball!"

A scruffy dog tore past, struggling to carry a lump of meat almost equal in size, shortly followed by the comical sight of Mr Banga, the butcher, trying desperately to keep up with it.

Albert laughed heartily to himself, and a thought occurred to him.

Other people would also have found that funny if they'd been there to see it. Many people. If only the moment could've been captured. Or… *recreated.*

He sketched a miniature Mr Banga chasing the four-legged thief inside the object's viewing window and wrote 'The Butcher's Dog' underneath, then scanned over the letter again. '*Magic trick of light*'… '*Small box, feeding big box*'.

Deep in thought for some time, he eventually returned to the drawing.

"How does it work?" he asked, tapping the quill against the side of his head. A word formed in his mind, and he transferred it neatly to the paper just above the box.

ALIGHTRIC

The driving rain came down in almost solid sheets, and strong gusts of wind seemed to attack from every direction. Even the horses were struggling to make headway. The driver could barely see ten feet ahead.

A pensive messenger sat in the comparative luxury of the carriage, with the grim reality of his upcoming task drawing nearer.

This is the worst thing I've ever had to do.

He could have sent Frank or a street officer, but the guilt-ridden chief felt he owed them this much at least.

After a while, the carriage came to a halt. Taking a deep breath, Lopez reluctantly opened the door and looked at the sign.

WELCOME TO BARLEYSO FARM

Mrs Brown eventually decided on a small bunch of yellow roses. She didn't know why, but the contrast between petals and thorns struck a chord.

"One sen, please."

"Thank you-ah."

"Beautiful day. Who's the lucky person, anyone special?"

"Jus' payin' me respecs."

"Oh, I'm sorry, I…"

"It's okay… jus' a friend. Thank you-ah."

"Thank you. Goodbye."

Fiona stood at the window and watched the old lady walk through the busy square.

Strolling the long stretch of riverside walkway, Mrs Brown stopped, at last, by the sign proudly announcing *Hamfist Way*. She carefully placed the roses against the bank wall beneath it, but her silent prayers were interrupted by a child running past in floods of tears.

"What's wrong, darling?" asked his mother.

"That nasty man scared me, Mummy. The man with the metal hat."

"He's not a nasty man," she laughed. "He's a Svelter… of The River Guard."

Pestilence walked alongside Death across a black, turbulent sky.

"Hope my time will come soon, Death."

"What? You want me to... y'know?" he replied, waving his scythe. "I'm not entirely sure it'll work, though— been having a few problems lately."

"No! Not that! I *mean* my time in the limelight."

"Time? I seem to remember your particular skills being called upon on many occasions."

"But nobody ever includes me in stories, fantastic tales, or even fantasies."

"Hmmm, I see your point."

"It *would* be nice to take part... just once."

"Maybe you should work on your profile...?"

Pestilence turned his 'face' to one side. "Like this?"

"... maybe not. Anyway, my old friend," Death said, shimmering slightly, "we seem to have been talking forever."

"Or maybe just a minute," replied Pestilence. "It's all just a matter of perspective."

THE BEGINNING...

When Victor was eventually ready to unleash his tactical mastery upon the world of stress, Brutus Stratus, quite blatantly, allowed the pry-minister to win.
The 'match' still lasted an incredible amount of time.

The good Gord giveth and the good Gord taketh away.
It's a cheap, dirty trick.

For Lawrence 'Lol' Whyatt… A fighter to the very end.

The Author

Chris Whyatt does not write epic fantasies.

While watching a 'movie' one day trying its utmost to fall into this category, a certain Mr Statham uttered the immortal line: "They are building an army of Gruggs!"—with an impressively straight face, Mr Whyatt unanimously agreed that 'epic' was best left to the experts. He chose to switch off at that point, but rest assured, somewhere along the line, it would also involve: "Only one thing can help us now… the sacred sword of… shield of… ring of… axe of… toothbrush of…"

In his short history as a writer, he has only ever made it to page ten before battle scenes, evil towers and rousing tavern songs are abandoned, and the humour creeps in.
That is *why* there are the Tolkiens (epic) of this world, the Pratchetts (humorous) of this world, and the Rowlings(?) of this world, leaving the utter Fantasy Outcasts to amuse themselves.
Chris Whyatt has to be pigeonholed somewhere, or the public won't know where to buy his stuff, and he'll have wasted years of his dubious existence. Unfortunately, upon searching, there is no category for 'Un-epic'. Come on, Amazon… sub-category?

Ta, like

Many thanks to Neil Gaiman for the best possible advice when I began my own little writing journey *and*... completely messed it up. Live. On social media.

"I'm sorry to hear that that happened. Start again, and don't worry. It's just Twitter (said a bit like "Forget it, Jake. It's Chinatown")."

Priceless.

Good friend, great writer, Rob Gregory... for invaluable help and advice.
I sincerely hope this book rewards him in *some* way.
I owe him at least a pint of Doom Bar and *possibly* a bag of peanuts.
If only he lived at the sensible end of the world or even a more accessible dimension.

In no way least, One Off Press... for all the usual stuff, but, most importantly, for having belief.
May your feathers never fall out and your well remain forever inky.

Did you enjoy this un-epic tale? No? Great! Please consider leaving a review.

More works of sub-greatness...

Barry & Ruffles: Phil Osafa's Stoned

Deadfool: Marbel's Uberheroes

Flame Tide: The Zeev Element

A Step Too VAR

Coming soon…

The second book in The Slightly Unfeasible Tales of Landos series and sequel to Svelt…

Eventful Times

Printed in Great Britain
by Amazon